Embracing
Dusty Detours

Text copyright © Lynne E. Chandler 2012
The author asserts the moral right
to be identified as the author of this work

Published by
The Bible Reading Fellowship
15 The Chambers, Vineyard
Abingdon OX14 3FE
United Kingdom
Tel: +44 (0)1865 319700
Email: enquiries@brf.org.uk
Website: www.brf.org.uk
BRF is a Registered Charity

ISBN 978 1 84101 829 4

First published 2012
10 9 8 7 6 5 4 3 2 1 0
All rights reserved

Acknowledgments
Unless otherwise stated, scripture quotations are taken from the Holy Bible, New International
Version, copyright © 1973, 1978, 1984 by International Bible Society, are used by permis-
sion of Hodder & Stoughton Publishers, a member of the Hachette Livre Group UK. All rights
reserved. 'NIV' is a registered trademark of International Bible Society. UK trademark number
1448790.

The paper used in the production of this publication was supplied by mills that source their
raw materials from sustainably managed forests. Soy-based inks were used in its printing and
the laminate film is biodegradable.

A catalogue record for this book is available from the British Library

Printed in Singapore by Craft Print International Ltd

Lynne E. Chandler

Embracing
Dusty Detours

A spiritual search
for depth in desert places

To my children,
Britelle and Treston
'*Gifts of life, I celebrate you.*'
∞ ✖ ∞

Acknowledgments

My thanks to…

*Tushar 'Tom' Zacharia and Barry Trowbridge.
Your spirits inspired so many;
you are deeply missed among us*

*My family: Paul-Gordon, Britelle and Treston,
fan club extraordinaire*

*Dad and Mom, for teaching me to see detours
as adventures, not dead ends*

*St John's music ensemble, book club and
the admirable people of Egypt,
for all you have given to me*

*My editor, Naomi Starkey, and all
the dedicated staff of BRF*

Contents

Foreword

We live at a moment of grace in which we are being invited to see, like humanity has never seen before, the interrelatedness of life, of our cultures and of our religious traditions. The question is whether we will meet this moment or miss it; whether we will be blessed by rediscovering our God-given interrelationship or cursed by denying it.

Lynne Chandler shows us the way of blessing. She does this by faithfully wrestling with some of the most ordinary events of family life and some of the most extraordinary events of the world today—life in Cairo. And all of this she does with a most poetic, beautiful and grace-filled spirit. This is a book of hope.

John Philip Newell
Former Warden of Iona Abbey
Author of A New Harmony: the Spirit, the Earth, and the Human Soul

Introduction

The idea of venturing off on a journey awakens a sense of anticipation and irresistible wonder in the heart of life-explorers. I was raised with powerful images from John Bunyan's classic book *The Pilgrim's Progress* lodged in my heart and mind. So much vivid imagery is woven into his 17th-century allegory. But the idea that I myself was journeying along a 'straight and narrow' path in life never seemed to reflect the reality of the twists and turns I was encountering along the way. Instead, the path I had somehow been launched upon was compelling and captivating in its own right, yet full of detours, short cuts and dead ends. J.R.R. Tolkien's intriguing tale of the journey of Bilbo Baggins in *The Hobbit* captivated my imagination at a young age and was a favourite book to be read aloud to us by my father when my brother and I were young. It gave me courage and a sense that the journey of life is about the details of wandering, not just the arrival.

However, my move to the chaotic city of Cairo, home to over 20 million people, some years ago did not lift me into the pages of a Tolkien adventure, but rather thrust me into the belly of a deep dark whale, alongside Jonah. Just after 9/11, I left the beauty of the north-western US, to become the music director of the Anglican/Episcopal international church in Cairo that my husband had been asked to pastor. The thought of moving to a giant, dirty city was terrifying. I didn't know how I could live without quietness or without being able to feed on God's beautiful creation. Usually our worst nightmares don't come true, but mine did. I loved our church community from day one, but this big city full of chaos, dust, smog and concrete just didn't work for me.

I cried for the first 18 months because God's voice had disappeared within me, and then I realised that my negative attitude was choking me to death. I decided that was not an option and I wanted to survive, but I never dreamed I would thrive. As I began the process of searching within, I found unexpected wells of refreshing water, the deeper I dug. My Creator met me where I was, and sustained me and restored me to a place of happiness and fulfilment that I'd never experienced. Many of those stories found their way into my first book, *Embracing a Concrete Desert: A spiritual journey towards wholeness*.

Emotionally I felt as if I'd climbed to the top of a huge mountain, and I wanted to enjoy the view. Yet even from the vantage point of a mountain top, life still plays on in all its colours. Exploring twists and turns, swamps and fields, deserts and valleys has awakened my heart to truly live. Like feeling the gift of the sun's warm rays when it manages to break through thick Cairo smog, I sense at last that I am embracing the present moment of life. I haven't arrived; I'm just resting, resting beside quiet waters that inevitably churn and stir from time to time and turn into strong currents that drag me back into the river of the hectic everyday.

Raw honesty has revealed a path into my own interior, where I can meet both myself and my Creator. It has helped me navigate what lies within and ensures that the hopes and dreams and fears I am carrying around don't remain hidden and unnamed. Longing to live from the foundation of my being, I stumble on, searching for sources of courage and strength waiting to carry me along the dusty detours of the path of life.

Launching fear

Now that I've committed myself to print, volumes of un-expected repercussions have presented themselves. Unlike my husband, Paul-Gordon, who felt that holding his first pub-lished book in his hands was like holding one of our newborn babies, I am gearing up for a personal natural disaster—some-thing akin to a time bomb cleverly concealed in a papyrus basket, which has floated down the Nile River to my doorstep, containing criticism so vast that the High River Dam would barely be able to hold back its torrent. Rather than facing my fear of rejection by a worldwide reading populace, I am on the run once again. Why can't I face it? What's the worst that could possibly happen?

Although I am among dear friends at my monthly church book club, the thought that we will soon be reading and dis-cussing my own first book has launched a new panic attack. It hadn't really crossed my mind that writing is a vulnerable endeavour until last month, when our usually mild-mannered book club hacked apart the most sweet and sincere book. Never in my wildest dreams would I have imagined that this little book could be so controversial. It is one of the rare works written that does not have a single negative online review to its name. How could my lovely, intelligent, generous friends turn on it in such a rage of vocal contempt? I was the one who started the discussion, with 'I liked this book but...' and then the 'but' grew into monstrous capital letters as my fellow readers pounced on the open window of 'BUT' and elaborated copiously. Thankfully our time together allows for diversions from the book at hand, which can lead to welcoming outbursts of uncontrollable laughter among friends.

But, as the dust settled, the looming release of my own nascent book zoomed into focus and I projected myself forward to the day of its official discussion. Perhaps I could just say outright, 'No criticism allowed' or 'Should I leave the room while you discuss this?' Visions of early musical recital disasters jumped to mind and stiffened my fingers with the memory of failed notes on the piano, and harp strings that refused to be plucked. Thankfully my teachers were usually kindhearted and would not verbally acknowledge the changes I'd made to well-known classical pieces. I was usually my own worst critic—but I didn't expect to get off so lightly the day I met a professional cathedral carillon bell ringer.

I had always been attracted to large musical instruments, and inside the bell tower of the cathedral we were attending in the US at the time lay a fascinating monstrous musical opportunity. As destiny would have it, the carilloneur was looking for a back-up performer so that she could take holidays when needed. Unlike the change-ringing bells in many UK cathedrals, these carillon bells are sounded from a clavier on which levers are arranged in sequence, like a piano keyboard or a harp. All that is involved is the striking of levers with fists and/or feet to direct clappers against the bells—fairly straightforward, I thought. After weeks below ground in the crypt, practising on the 49 bells of a mock instrument, I was deemed ready to be released on the surrounding neighbourhood for a live attempt from the bell tower. Up the constricted tower I climbed for the first time and, when I emerged from the final ladder, I stood enthralled by the wooing presence of 'Big John', the largest cast bell, weighing in at more than 2000 pounds.

A brief orientation was necessary before I carefully arranged my music and waited for my instructor to scramble back downstairs to find a better listening vantage point. Then I began to play. Loud peals rang from each bell I engaged, echoing straight into my brain and shooting my adrenalin into overdrive; panic was not an option. I braced myself and plunged forward into the music, trying to ignore the fact that I was missing most of the bells I had spent weeks ringing below. Soon, to my surprise, the resonating sound waves pulsing around me seemed to be blurring harmonically. I relaxed slightly, finished my short repertoire and then waited nervously for my instructor to climb back up to my hunchbacked haven and berate my performance. Finally she emerged from the narrow ladder, but with a very wide smile on her face. Contrary to my worst imaginary fears, her constructive criticism included words such as 'A brilliant first try' and 'However did you manage to skip most of the written notes in your score and still make it sound so beautiful?' Phew. Beginner's luck?

Maybe I'll have such luck with my potentially short-lived writing career. However, a book is not a musical instrument. Its pages are etched with indelible print, for ever, in black and white. It will not be possible to pretend that what someone has criticised is not there. I wonder how those political spin doctors learn their trades: maybe there's something there I can learn! Or I could just break down and cry, or pretend I don't speak the language, or both. That helped me once in Tunisia when I found myself in trouble with the law. I had innocently parked my car outside a new grocery store, along with a dozen other vehicles, but I hadn't realised that it was in an illegal sand-and-dirt car park. I don't know how the other drivers fared but, as I returned to my car, juggling bags and my tired children, I got read the riot act by a very large policeman with a very loud French voice. My three-year-old daughter, Britelle, watched anxiously while my six-month-old son, Treston, started wailing loudly. Despite my bravest efforts, I started to cry, mumbling and bumbling about how hard it was to be a foreigner in his country. I'm sure he couldn't understand a word I was saying, and he got disgusted, threw my driver's licence back through the window at me and didn't even attempt to get a bribe. (I'm not saying he would have...)

Fear: it's an attention-grabbing emotion. What is its presence telling me? As a risk-taker, I can usually move through fear more readily than I do through many of the emotions in my daily inventory. When all else fails, I remind myself that although I'm afraid of heights, I willingly joined friends at age 20 to parachute from 3000 feet in the air, for fun. It was fun, but I'm still afraid of heights. However, the fear of failure is an even more powerful force. There is no promise of fun involved in the embracing process, just the threat of looming humiliation. Perhaps if I faced it, I could learn from it? Maybe. Could failure be as horribly incapacitating as the fear of failure? Possibly.

Yet, when I do allow life to be my muse, I stop resisting the gift of today and listen, pay attention, wonder. I realign myself with my deepest desires, the God-given desires of my heart. That may even mean being launched once again from a comfort zone of sunny warmth and security, to find a whole new venture awaiting my consent. I may conceivably survive my book's launching after all. The shores of the Nile River may not overflow and swallow me whole. The ticking bomb in the papyrus basket may indeed turn out to be some sort of newborn baby experience in disguise. I suppose, at this point, when indelible ink has set its course, it is what it is—a bit of me shared and, I hope, a connection with someone else on the journey, reducing the distance between us and helping to cheer one another on.

When the dreaded day of our book club discussion arrived, I found I was among kindred spirits, some relating directly to the challenging transition to life in Cairo, and others telling of their own 'concrete deserts'—from difficult relationships to health issues, to grieving the loss of a loved one. Kindly, the only 'negative' comment expressed was that the book ended too soon, without a wrapped-up happily-ever-after ending, but rather as a journey still in process.

An unruly voice

Fear: sometimes an
Unruly voice,
If invited to speak
It destroys.

With no respect for a higher vision
It can darken the brightest of days.

Its bitter taste can undermine
The risk of
Hopes and dreams.

Its scent can smother
And choke out courage,
Slamming an open door shut.

But if only acknowledged
And not asked to stay,
This wanderer
Must move on.

When the tangible touch
Of fear starts to fade
The gift of trust can emerge.

Edges of our beings

One sunny afternoon in Cairo, my husband pointed out to me how dirty one section of our living-room curtain was, because it was situated in front of the air conditioning wall unit for that room. Because of its location, it was impossible for it to avoid collecting polluted outside air, being cooled on its way in. 'That's just part of being a curtain in Cairo,' I responded. By that I meant the obvious: the curtain is inevitably going to be dirty, regardless of how often we clean the filter of the air conditioning unit. My husband laughed and probably made a mental note to clean it at another time; and I felt triumphant that at least I wouldn't have to face any extreme curtain clean-up myself.

But of course, in the end, I didn't let myself off the hook. I wasn't about to try to clean the uncleanable, but I did start driving myself crazy by analysing the spiritual significance of my statement. Maybe I had been alone too long that day. This was the first year I had consciously carved out a 'writing day', which seemed too good to be true. With all the other respon-sibilities that swirled around the life of our church commu-nity, it felt almost selfish, yet still necessary. I had quite a few tries to get it right, to treat myself to as much silence as Cairo and my living-room could offer. Armed with a journal and my favourite pen, I had no idea how hard it would be to guard a mere six sacred hours of time for writing. First a phone call, which I could have ignored but didn't; then a building guard knocking on the door in need of something, which I couldn't have ignored so didn't. Then my piano started staring at me from the other side of the room, taunting me that I had better not skip a day of practice, or else. Yet my writing day is evolving into something that I can't compromise if I want to keep my own 'filter' clean. It's a time of feeding and listening, creating and giving, receiving and recording. Some days it may produce something visible and other days something invisible. It's the invisible that I am trying to access and tap into—and that takes time and quiet, with no distractions.

Today I am in need of a full security-guard detail. I look over at my old faithful dog, who is flat out, snoozing deeply. She's hired. 'Pepsi, you have been promoted, at age 84 in dog years, to guard the writing day. Do not let anyone prise me from my spot. Keep sleeping if you must, but be on alert.' She is resting so completely that I have to make sure I can see the Pepsi-coloured fur on her chest rising and falling. She's certainly not just sleeping from the edges of her being. Then the doomed dirty curtain behind me starts staring, burrowing into my brain like the stone gaze of the Sphinx in Giza. Will this day ever progress? I break down and clean it.

Back to writing: I have become obsessed with the concept of living from the foundation of my being, rather than on the edges. There is something about the core of our beings that pulls like a magnet, as if there is an anchor at the centre of our souls where God keeps everything in balance. It takes intention and time to peel back the layers and see what lies within.

I love the fact that I cannot fully comprehend God. I love the fact that the concept of eternity is beyond me. It grounds me in mystery. It assures me that this life is far beyond the borders of my own personal existence. All is well. Maybe not yesterday or tomorrow, but, in the grand scope of things, I must trust. All is well right now, in this present moment.

Life is not just happening to us. It is being guided overall with a loving, tender care that far surpasses what we would give our own children. This is not a demanding parent we are dealing with, who wants or needs to control every detail; this is God. We have a say in our choices; we have a part in writing the stories of our lives. Maybe we've been given the setting or the characters but we do have some say in the twists and turns of the plot. When life requires decisions that could send us in the opposite direction to our current situation, what will motivate our choices? What has motivated our choices in the past? Step back. Step within. There we will find what we want to see happen, the true voice of our heart's desires. Without a vision for our present or a longing for our future, we may end up standing still, lingering without courage and letting life just happen to us. Sometimes we have no options; sometimes we have many. Every day we have the freedom to choose to complain. Every day we have the freedom to choose to celebrate.

Life, in relation to the rhythm of our inner beings, can set us free to be truly ourselves. To live from the original pattern of our souls, from the infinite treasure resting at the depths of our beings, will root us deeply, to withstand any storm that life brings our way. To enter into the place of stillness that has always been, yet is not of our own making, is to allow our souls to be centred by God. In that deepest part of ourselves, we know that the current of life runs deeper than death.

I love the gift of perspective woven into Celtic spirituality —the belief that what is deepest in us is the image of God. Although that image has been blurred, it is not erased. Layers may have built up over and around it, but God's grace can reconnect us to that presence at our core, if only we will ask and then journey.

It will be a journey made just for you. Every gift will be provided, according to your needs. Let go of all the layers that entangle your soul. God's Spirit is in the wind and God's voice will come to you in the silent hours of the night. Listen. Follow. Be present in the moment. As close and intimate as your own breath, as far and vast as the great night sky, God is present, now and always. God's will and our own inner dreams can coincide. There is a thread of purpose woven into the fabric of our very beings. There is a path for each of us.

In search of You

In search of You,
My deepest
Longing,
From my first breath
Until now.

Some days it's been
A conscious journey
Along a well-planned path.

Other days it's only
Been in response
To the pulsing wind
Of your Spirit.

Never forced, always present,
My very own breath;
You've woven a path for me.

Since the dawn of time,
Within and without,
Longing,
I search for You.

Lazarus

My husband, Paul-Gordon, was in the midst of preaching a sermon at our church in Cairo, on the New Testament parable of the rich man and Lazarus (Luke 16). Interestingly, its origins are in an ancient Egyptian folk tale, and Paul-Gordon reminded us that this was the only time when Jesus gave a name to a character in any of his parables. A 'poor beggar' is the only person given a name (a very important honour in this Middle Eastern context): 'Lazarus', meaning 'the one whom God helps or heals'. He explained that Jesus' version of this story tells us that God is just and merciful and compassionate. God sees and will ultimately take care of the Lazaruses of this world, and we are invited to join in that caring.

As my husband was nearing the end of his sermon, a visiting woman in the front row started crying. At first I assumed she had been touched by something he had said, but soon the crying turned into heavy, inconsolable weeping. Ending his sermon early, Paul-Gordon went over to try to comfort her. He gently asked if she would follow him outside so that he could help her, but she immediately started screaming, 'I don't want to talk to you!' Her hostility and her obvious fear of something we could not see escalated as she shrieked uncontrollably. I had no idea what to do. No one had any idea what to do. Then our resourceful Nigerian property manager, Kingsley, came down the aisle to help. After her hands had been forcibly but carefully prised away from the pew, he scooped her up with superhuman strength and carried her out of the church. Immediately several others went out with them. What followed was the outplaying of the powerful principles of compassionate care just spoken of in the sermon. Our church community was swept into action, as if by instinct.

Thankfully, the children were out at Church School at the time and, intuitively, several trained educators left the worship service to make sure they didn't return until all was safe. I left the piano briefly to explain the situation to the teachers, as an entirely self-appointed team from the congregation joined together to facilitate the woman's care. Our assistant minister had done an internship at a psychiatric hospital while at training college, so seemed to have some idea about what was taking place. A nurse, who had been sitting right next to the visitor, was invaluable, as were so many others. As this broken woman was sheltered in a nearby room until her caretakers could arrive, we were led in a prayer, full of the knowledge of God's loving care for her, before continuing on into Communion together.

The incident really shook us up as a community. We were drained and exhausted, like a family that had just received a shock. We were very grateful that the woman had been in the safe haven of our church family when her breakdown took place. It was a poignant living illustration of what the day's scripture readings were communicating. Reaching out in love to someone in need, our congregation bonded together to show grace and compassion. I could easily picture Jesus being present. I'm sure his Middle Eastern culture offered many such opportunities to help. With what love and strength his heart would have reacted—and, knowing the deepest part of her, he would have known what to do, what to say. In the rawness of this woman's violent vulnerability we received a glimpse into a world I had not experienced so tangibly before. She was created and loved, as were we, by her Creator, completely.

My first conscious attraction to the idea of community came to me at the age of 17, while I was revisiting the jungles of the second largest rainforest in the world, the Ituri Forest. This stretched canopy of green giants in north-eastern Congo guarded inaccessible trees from extinction and sheltered the friends I had traversed the globe to meet: pygmies, lepers and a Canadian nurse. Ten summers had passed since I had been uprooted from Africa's soil to follow my parents to the US. My family had lived in a rural town with occasional ventures into the forest for exploration and adventure. Vibrant butterflies, lush waterfall pools and communities of pygmies captivated my imagination—then and now.

Dodging muddy ruts and holes one afternoon, the Canadian nurse's aged vehicle manoeuvred us over forest roads en route to the ceremonial occasion of a great tree-felling. The Bantu pygmy community had spent days battling the giant with crude axes, slowly whittling its width, promising triumph. Appraising the size of the chosen tree required seven open-armed adults to encircle its girth. Trajectory predictions were announced by pygmy warriors balancing on makeshift scaffolding secured to the enormous trunk. Just as the tree began its fatal sway, they jumped from harm's way. Crack. Snap. Boom. A pounding echo shook the earth beneath my feet; the monster was felled. We ran to climb on the massive trunk, until a victim screamed of attack: driver ants were pouring from the log. We dived off the demolished dwelling of this fierce ant kingdom and jumped around, shaking ourselves free. A contagious ripple of laughter ensued, linking us to the celebrating community.

I returned from my African summer with a new appreciation for the connection of community. Memories—holding a smiling leper's disintegrating hand in a jungle clinic, and sharing monkey stew in a tribal chief's home—challenged my independent manner. I was part of a community in the US, but it had a splintered look to it: family, friends, school, church. My heart was rooted in my church at that time, which carved out safe places for me to thrive and be nourished. My appreciation was perhaps minimal then, but the foundation it set in place provided a solid refuge as time went on. Hardships hit my life and storms blew through, while laughter and joy mingled with tears and pain.

Close-knit communities have surprised me each time I have lived in a foreign context. Although the dusty Middle Eastern city of Cairo has proved to be the greatest of challenges, it has also given me the most fulfilling moments of my life. I attribute this paradox to community, as well as God's lavish doses of grace. Alongside other expatriates, the energy of survival, the need for companionship and the realisation that we are journeying through an exotic adventure together continually breaks down barriers. Our international church includes dozens of nationalities and many different denominations. Rather than producing conflicting opinions of how things should be done, it throws its members together in appreciation of an oasis from the pressures of life. Though many of my Egyptian Muslim friends may never set foot inside our church doors, they have welcomed me with wide-open hearts. The edges of my traditional sense of community have been pushed and transformed to embrace a feeling of interconnection far beyond the borders of creed and culture.

Whenever I limit my focus to my own needs, they grow out of proportion. Whenever I open myself to the needs of others, my own traumas soften and I sense the oneness that my Creator must have intended all along. Many a mother here in my city cannot meet the needs of her hungry children; although I have not experienced that, I have had my own desperate moments in life that have choked out all hope. An unemployed father feels imprisoned by the unjust cycle of poverty; although I have not experienced that, I have been trapped in emotional prisons that have threatened the depths of my being.

I have much to learn from the strength that these others draw from their own communities. It seems to be most purely reflected in a rural village setting here in Egypt, where traditional life nurtures interdependence with one another: fathers need daughters, grandmothers need grandsons, and nephews and nieces need uncles. When economic devastation forces them to trade fresh country air for big city pollution, the vigour of community is threatened. They flounder to fit into new communities; the trauma of uprooting is evident. Where two people once shared a rural home, now ten are crammed into one dark room with no plumbing or electricity. Our church, alongside the wider community, has found meaningful ways to contribute to relieving the suffering around us. The dedication I see in these efforts pours wholeness into my soul.

Being a part of the church community often reminds me of family. The intimacy that can develop in such a context is not forced but natural. Some days it's just there and I am an unseen part of it; other days it's there and I am fully conscious of it and thankful to belong. The church is a chosen community, washed with purpose and held in a divine embrace. We have a relational rather than just a functional sense of identity: we are part of something larger than ourselves. It is forgiving, as a family must be if it is to weather life's storms, every part working to sustain every other part. Moving from being a group of independent people with a common interest, we can grow together towards being a force of outwardly focused people, travelling together and celebrating God. We desire to express and reflect God's love and image, planted in the centre of our beings. By investing in and journeying with others, we learn what it means to be a part of God's heart, connected in authentic loving ways and engaged in transparent relationships that cultivate and celebrate Christ's love. If I cannot see the handprint of God in the life of another, it is because my vision is blurred: too many layers have covered my heart's sensor. When this happens, I need to step back and rest in a still quiet place. Only here will I find the living water that flows freely and restores my soul.

When I first moved to Cairo, a spiritual sandstorm swallowed me (as I described in *Embracing a Concrete Desert*). Exchanging lush, quiet fields and natural landscapes that fed my soul for a noisy, crowded and dirty metropolis was traumatic. I sensed God's voice growing fainter as layers of smog clogged my heart and blotted out hope. I was a most unlikely candidate for survival, due to my loathing of large city settings, yet I think that was part of the point. I guess my new community didn't need somebody to sweep in and master concrete desert living with flair. It needed me to stumble along, to be honest, to question, to bargain, to beg, and to cry until nothing was left.

One summer, while I was regrouping with my family back in the US, someone asked me, 'Is there anyone you feel you can let your hair down with in Egypt?' The question took me aback. Did they suppose I was holding out on people? Maybe they though I was pretending all was well? 'My hair is always down,' I replied. If it wasn't, I would have missed out on community building: listening, upholding, comforting, encouraging, empathising, learning, growing and finding the best in each other.

When all else fails in my modus operandi, I remember to look at Jesus. That's when genuine growth takes place. My lurching record of development might look appalling if plotted on a graph, but Christ's life gives me hope every time I seek strength in the truth of his stories. Just think of the story of Lazarus, in which a needy, homeless man is bestowed with the honourable gift of a beautiful name. The name Jesus gave him reflects pure goodness at the depth of God's character: 'the one who God helps or heals'. It is a story that keeps on living. It is full of forever.

Full of forever

Full of forever,
Your story keeps speaking
To the deepest
Part of me.

Full of forever,
A faded memory
Begins to grow
Within.

Full of forever,
I hear your voice speaking
Through the life
Of a trusted friend.

Full of forever,
I see your eyes calling
Through the face
Of a passing stranger.

Full of forever,
Communion, compassion,
Grace, strength,
Love.

Full of forever,
You hold your creation.
Your arms
Encircle the earth.

Triumphal entry

Since moving to the Middle East, I have developed a bit of an obsession with donkeys. What sort of image comes to mind when you think of a donkey: gloomy Eeyore, Sancho Panza's faithful 'Rucio', Pinocchio's naughty boys, children's rides at fairgrounds or on the beach? If you are born a donkey in Upper Egypt, you are usually a bit fluffy-looking, clean and happy. If you are born in Cairo, well, you are at best hero-ically sustaining someone's livelihood. During our first few years in Cairo, donkeys were an integral part of managing our daily rubbish collection. Eventually the city's authorities de-cided that our dear donkeys and their carts were a nuisance to the growing car population, so the welcome sound of clip-clop, clip-clop was banned from our neighbourhoods. But occasional glimpses still remain, and our church supports a wonderful life-giving donkey care project run by a visionary Muslim veterinarian here, whose sole passion is to train fami-lies to treat their donkeys respectfully as part of God's cre-ation. With humane harnesses, basic health care and training in how to care for their needs, the donkeys' longevity gives back so much more to the families who depend on them for their very existence, carrying rubbish for recycling or hauling loads of vegetables to market.

I visited Jerusalem for the first time recently and replayed every Bible story I had ever read in my mind with a new lens in place: the 'triumphal entry' of Jesus into Jerusalem, for instance. If I had been on the triumphal entry planning committee, I don't think I would have voted for a donkey to carry Jesus, despite my current fixation. Why not upgrade to an Arab stallion? Now there is triumph and drama—a commanding presence, for sure. I suppose, in those days, however, the riding of a stately horse was reserved for powerful kings and army officials. Perhaps riding a donkey was like borrowing a VW Beetle for a parade. Walking would definitely not have been memorable on such an occasion: after the ascent up the hill to Jerusalem, Jesus would have entered the walled city gate looking like everyone else just milling about. However, the fact that a wave of human interest fanned out along the route, upon the appearance of Jesus on his borrowed donkey, is news enough. A word-of-mouth announcement still spreads like wildfire here in the Middle East.

Have you ever seen a grown man riding a donkey? The image is still very much alive here in the Middle Eastern countryside and ancient cities alike. It is actually an endearing sight, even if not very triumphal. You can't help but wonder if the poor donkey's back is sagging beyond repair from the added weight, not to mention the awkward balancing act involved, with human legs dangling so closely to the ground. Apparently donkeys can carry 20 to 30 per cent of their own body weight. I wonder how much donkeys weigh? I'm sure an underweight man wouldn't cause too much trauma—but still…

I love the raw imagery preserved in so many stories of the Bible. It doesn't seem to have gone through a sanitising editorial process, sweeping all the ordinariness of everyday life under a carpet. It is alive to the senses. The delightful Old Testament story of the random prophet Balaam and his ever so spiritually-in-tune donkey companion is a triumph for donkeys everywhere. An angel of the Lord is sent to warn Balaam that he has made a really bad choice in life, and only the donkey sees the angel blocking their way on a road toward certain death. The donkey even gets to talk in the rendition that our ancient text has preserved for us through the ages (Numbers 22:21–41).

Donkeys: we imagine one carrying a pregnant Mary on her way to Bethlehem, looking on during the miraculous birth of Jesus in the manger, sustaining the holy family during their flight to Egypt, and then, later in Jesus' life, taking part in the 'triumphal entry'. The triumphal entry into Jerusalem signals the end of the beginning in the life of Jesus, amid the shouts of 'Hosanna; blessed is he who comes in the name of the Lord!' (Matthew 21:9). Yet that beginning, that coming, is in some senses still taking place, as every day the sun comes up and announces that God's presence is at hand. Light breaks through the veil of mystery dividing earth and heaven whenever we have eyes to see and ears to hear.

I don't think these biblical stories were documented for a one-time information-gathering read. These stories are alive: they breathe; they replay. They bring us hope and strength and courage. These stories have been told again and again and again. The triumphal power of God was present in the very essence of Jesus when the privileged yet ordinary donkey carried him into Jerusalem to the waving of palms and the reverence of cloaks placed in his path. It is a story to savour, to ponder, to draw strength from, and to recognise when a retelling makes an appearance in our own lives.

On a donkey

I hang on the stories
Told of You.
Were You cold
That day long ago?

Did flies bite Your ankles
Or stray dogs bark
As You rode into town
On a donkey?

Could Your warm melting smile
Be seen in Your eyes,
Or was pain
Battling with joy?

Were You hungry or thirsty?
Were Your feet sore from walking
When You climbed on the
Young colt's back?

Was he afraid to be ridden?
Did he know it was You?
Did he calm to the
Touch of Your presence?

Pentecost

Where should I begin? 'My African dog ate the Pentecost dove.' No, too cruel. My dog is a loving creature. She would never hurt a fly. Well, maybe I have seen her skilfully snap up a few insufferable flies in her time.

It was Thursday evening—'Pentecost Eve', as our Holy Day here in Egypt is Friday. Paul-Gordon and I had returned from leading a reflective evening worship service. The meditative songs were still quietly replaying in my head. Earlier that day my husband had made the annual pilgrimage to the local bird store, to pick up the pure white dove he had ordered in advance. It was always an exciting moment for our family each year when he returned home with the Pentecost bird, full of life and meaning and wonder. We would inspect its feathers to make sure it was actually pure white, as, the first time we decided to inaugurate this tradition, our requested white dove was sprinkled with black feathers and the bird shop owner had to rush to secure a last-minute white substitute. Once Paul-Gordon had explained to the birdman that this was like needing a pure white sheep for the Muslim feast of *Eid Al Adha*, then naturally only white birds appeared.

It had become a special tradition to release a dove in the church garden at the end of our Pentecost Day service, in celebration of the Holy Spirit's coming, and that ongoing presence in our lives. Actually the 'dove' was always a pure white homing pigeon, able to fly straight home and avoid city hawks on its route. Having raised birds in Africa as a child,

Paul-Gordon's enthusiasm for these feathered friends was catching. He would hold the bird carefully for the children to see during the worship service Children's Time and explain about God's Spirit and the symbolism of the dove. Last year, the first question he asked the children was, 'What does this bird remind you of?' Immediately a little boy's hand shot up with the answer: 'Jesus Christ.' (That seems to be the standard answer that they fall back on when unsure.) Thankfully the little boy wasn't asked to expound theologically but his inspiration was woven into the lesson. After explaining how we would all be saying some words together later about the coming of God's Spirit, before releasing the dove in the garden, the final question my husband asked was, 'Does anyone know what we will say when we release this dove?' Another hand shot up: 'Goodbye?' These astute children keep us on our toes!

Back to Thursday evening: it was well past 11pm when our daughter burst into our room in a panic: 'Where's the Pentecost bird?' 'In a box in the office,' my husband replied as he rushed past me out of the door. We arrived to a scene of countless white feathers and our big gentle dog, Pepsi, cowering in the corner looking suspiciously like the cat that swallowed the canary. The bird's box was tipped over on to the floor; it was gone. Could Pepsi have swallowed it whole? She looked dreadfully confused and afraid. I refused to prise open her jaws and look for evidence. We searched high and low. No sign of the bird, only feathers all over the floor. I didn't know whether to laugh or cry. Being a vegetarian, it was beyond me to imagine that my own pampered pup could succumb to her inbred hunting dog instincts and annihilate an ancient Christian symbol.

We eventually found the little winged creature, hiding in a corner of our apartment, still alive but visibly not long for this world. Then I cried. My husband was being more practical and, in anxiety, realised that it was now 11.30pm and he had to have a Pentecost dove in hand before our morning service. The bird shop was closed and would not open until after midday prayers the following day. Since Egypt is a night culture, however, there was still a chance to track down a pigeon fancier in an apartment roof-top loft and beg for help.

An hour later, Paul-Gordon returned, beaming with success and carrying a gorgeous pure white bird (double the usual price), having risked life and limb climbing up a rickety homemade ladder to a tenth-floor loft, but now boasting of the bird's aerobatic tumbling talents in addition to its homing instincts.

I remembered seeing such athletic birds in the *khan* (market) in old Islamic Cairo one evening at sunset. I was exploring the roof-top of a building being renovated and looked across the way to see a man exercising his pigeons. The entire time, he stood on his own roof-top near the entrance of his pigeon loft, whistling signals and waving a white flag. His birds soared above in the dusk sky, practising winged formations, tumbling, and circling the neighbourhood, flying freely. Eventually their owner called them in with a distinctive whistle and wave of his flag. I was spellbound.

Now we had been rescued by the presence of such a bird. Pentecost was saved. Our children were sworn to secrecy until the Pentecost send-off had been successfully launched, and no one was any the wiser the next morning, as the 'dove' flew powerfully into the air after the congregation had prayed together, 'Come, Holy Spirit. Fill our hearts and kindle in us the fire of your love.' I haven't dared to ponder the symbolic significance of the whole event, but it will certainly be a Pentecost to remember.

Your promised gift arrives

Fire, wind, whirling voices
A sensing of your power.

New-found courage,
Strength and hope,
Your promised gift arrives.

Timeless imagery,
Dove of peace,
Living symbols of love.

Yet for all these gifts
I would rather experience
Your physical presence, Lord.

To trust, to follow,
To be led through the shadows
By the guiding grace of your hand.

Some days the path brings
More questions than answers,
As emotional earthquakes engulf.

Some days the light
Shines down so brightly.
A quiet voice whispers my name.

Still present,
Your sacred energy fills
My being and wills me to live.

Graduation

Two days before graduation: I'm practising my crying again for my daughter's high school graduation ceremony this week. Do I need to bring along one full box of tissues or two? I keep vacillating. Paul-Gordon is giving the benediction prayer, a Muslim sheik the invocation. The backdrop of the ceremony will be the Sphinx and the Great Pyramids of Giza. Perhaps it's best that my husband will be up on stage, rather than beside me. Otherwise I probably wouldn't be able to hold things together, and how embarrassing that would be for my remaining teenage son next to me.

It all keeps coming in waves: happiness, sadness, relief, admiration, thankfulness. Just the flickering thought of projecting myself forward a few days and hearing the first bars of 'Pomp and Circumstance' bellow out from the sound system gives me images of being able to hire myself out as a Middle Eastern mourning wailer. Hopefully it won't come to that, but I'm really not sure. And my tears are as much about joy as sadness: joy in celebrating all that she has become, overwhelmingly blessed beyond my highest hopes and dreams; sadness in losing a daily physical presence, a part of myself, a soul I have watered for so many years and will continue to water from afar. To step back and look at this beautiful flowering miracle before my eyes reminds me of the day when she was born. I stand in awe of her Creator.

Today I wrote out my graduation card to her. That was what started this messy episode of reflection. I thought I had processed everything already in my weeping session several weeks back, but I think I'm still moving forward. Thankfully I have other friends who are with me in the same phase of life. The ones who have gone before me give me hope: they are still walking upright. The ones going through the send-off of their firstborn babies with me give me comfort. We are in this together. We will survive. We will listen to each other's stories. We will cry together and then begin to revive, to find ourselves not empty but full as we see our children growing into their wings, soaring where even we have not soared.

However will I face sending off my other baby? Thank goodness I have a reprieve for three years. Will I cling to him possessively and mercilessly? I have absolutely zero recollection of thinking that this milestone moment was hard on my parents, way back when. I remember my mother always telling me to keep my hands open—speaking figuratively, about my heart—not grasping a gift as if it was all and only mine. It's hard not to succumb, though. I must remember what a grace it is that the world lies before my own daughter now. She is ready.

One day before graduation: today I drafted my daughter's 'leaving the family nest for college' letter. My father wrote me one, and its significance still lingers with strength in my memory. I can't believe how fast time has flown by. To have been entrusted with this cherished gift, who has now bloomed into a young adult, is bewilderingly beautiful. Before I fully let go, I'm racking my brain in search of any important last-minute lessons I may have missed, besides ironing and sewing on buttons. I wasn't one for last-minute cramming for school exams, so hopefully I haven't missed anything major. What have I been trying to communicate to her all these last years? I suppose it's the same thing God has been communicating to me: 'God goes with you every step, every moment of every day, now and always. You have so much beauty inside you to give; it is a well that will never run dry. God's image shines so brightly in you and you innately see this in others.'

This last Mother's Day, she wrote me the most moving words on a photo she had taken of an experience we had shared together in nature last summer. Her lyrical words expressed how she may sometimes forget my words but will never forget the tune. She has been breathing life into my song, my life, these many years. That tune has now joined her own melody and is part of the harmony beneath her wings, a melody that will soar on as she explores the heights and depths of the life she's been given.

Free to be

Follow the light
That is drawing you forward,
Trust the source of its rhythm.

Soar and explore
The great tapestry of time,
Weave threads of your own on the way.

Melodies sing
The song of your life,
Calling you on toward freedom,

While notes of harmony
Mingle throughout,
Breathing life into treasured moments.

A design, a melody,
A harmony within
Will turn every step to dancing.

Each moment you live
Has chosen you,
With sacred beauty and purpose.

It's time to fly
Where dreams are leading,
Enjoying the gift of life.

Open hearts, open hands,
Your course is set.
At last, you are free
To be.

Gebel Musa

Moses is a local 'saint' here among Christians and Muslims, but I think he would look even more impressive if he was brought down out of the clouds and seen as an ordinary person. From what I saw on my one climb up the barren Sinai slopes, this guy was hardcore. I'm sure he gave himself more than one afternoon to make the pilgrimage to the top, but still... I even cheated, on my mountain trek, by taking a camel as my chauffeur most of the way. What a sight that was! Camel-back is not as luxurious a ride as you might imagine.

For years our family had been saving this trip to Mount Sinai (or *Gebel Musa*: 'mountain of Moses') for a special occasion, and my visiting in-laws gave us the perfect opportunity. I started gathering information, and stories were often mixed as to the degree of difficulty this pilgrimage would present. We wisely promised to reward ourselves with a few days of Red Sea snorkelling afterwards so that we could recover fully and enjoy some family time together.

Seeing that our ages ranged from 14 to 75, we decided to bypass the 3750 'Steps of Repentance' and pamper ourselves with the camel trail. To wind along the rocky sloping trail, riding high atop our own camel humps, seemed a dream come true. The journey up was absolutely spectacular. Breathtaking scenes of valleys, rugged mountain passes and hidden springs stretched out before us. Our Bedouin guides kept our camels on track with a variety of whistling and clicking signals. Railings to protect us from sheer cliff drops were non-existent, so, when our meandering camels shifted their weights from side to side near such vistas, we sat up straight and paid attention. Our guides corrected our posture, when needed, to perfect the balancing act on our 'desert ships'. I'd only ever ridden a camel for short distances before, so I had never really experienced the swaying, calming rhythm, so different from horseback riding. A camel's legs shift from right to left, right to left, until a surprising lilt lulls you into a trusting mode. They walk these mountain trails day and night, their whole lives. I had nothing to worry about on the way up.

The return ride down the mountain after sunset was impossible, however. What were we thinking? I vaguely remembered wondering, when we were bargaining our fare with the camel owners at the foot of the mountain range, why they had set a separate price for the ascent and descent. At first they assumed we were only riding up, but, once they understood our request, wide conniving eyes of understanding locked in silently among themselves, producing a major discount for the return journey. It became crystal clear to me many hours later, when my camel, named Sugar, lurched forward at a dangerous downward angle and rammed me into the front of my small Bedouin saddle. I immediately abandoned ship and chose to walk down. If we'd had a full moon, perhaps the walk would have been more enjoyable—or if we'd read the guidebooks more carefully and packed flashlights.

Britelle bolted off on her camel in front of me at the start of our descent, followed by my brave mother-in-law, and I could hear the echo of warnings being called out by my daughter: 'Bump', which meant 'lift and brace yourself'. They would make it down the mountain in record time. Their voices carried a mixture of laughter and moaning as they faded off into the night. Behind me, my husband's voice sounded tense but determined. His camel and guide endured many 'Stop immediately and let me off!' commands in Arabic and English. It shouldn't have made me smile, but it did. His guide would adjust his saddle in the dark and on he would climb again. Only later did we realise that these camels were not the same breed as the large Saharan Desert friends we were used to. They were mountain camels with very small saddles, suited perfectly for lean Bedouin teenagers. Some discoveries come the hard way! My father-in-law was the revered hero of the event, never uttering a single complaint; he readily admitted that he was too busy praying for our safety.

But back to the upward journey: after leaving our luggage in our rooms at St Catherine's Monastery, important keeper of the thriving descendant of the burning bush, and negotiating our transportation, we settled into the climb. We had debated whether to rise at 3am with other visiting pilgrims from around the world to climb up and see the sunrise together. But having come from the choking crowds of Cairo just that morning, we decided on a sunset visit instead. It was by far the quieter option and gave us a chance to soak in the views we were seeing while we and our camels were still fresh. The entire area we were climbing through was a protected reserve, going back at least as far as the prophet Mohammed's lifetime, when he declared the Christian monastery a safe haven and forbade any raiding attacks. The monastery still has his original signed edict on display.

About an hour into our ride, I could see the final 'steps' approaching in the distance. Several tour books I'd read expounded on the final ascent, accessible only by foot. It was rumoured that a donkey or two had made the journey successfully, but I can't imagine how. As the jagged valley below us grew smaller, we caravanned past an area called 'Elijah's Basin', marked by an old cypress tree next to a rock-lined pool of fresh water. I got so excited to see another Bible story brought to life. This is the place honoured historically as the one where God nourished the prophet Elijah with water from a brook, and sent ravens to feed him (1 Kings 17:1–6). The Old Testament records that these ravens brought him bread and meat in the morning and evening. Our Palestinian Christian friend, Archbishop Elias Chacour, told us that the Hebrew words for 'raven' and 'Bedouin' share the same consonants—and, as is the case in Arabic today, vowels were not recorded in the Hebrew scriptures. So perhaps Elijah was actually fed by Bedouins, not ravens. Regardless of which vowels win out, however, in that setting it was clearly a miraculous intervention.

Eventually my camel signalled that the riding portion of the journey was over. He snorted, shook his head and suddenly pitched me forward, then jolted me backward and ended his routine by folding up his legs underneath him. By then I had mastered the technique of holding on tightly to the front *and* back of my saddle. I dismounted with great care as a cliff plunged downward just steps away. Where was the railing? Where were my children?

Only a mere 750 uneven red granite steps remained. I had been told there were both a mosque and a small Greek Orthodox chapel on the summit site, the highest point in the Sinai region. I was excited to be near the top but just a bit nervous, too, because I don't like heights. I could see my children already racing for the steps, so off I followed. Just minutes into my climb I started to get extremely dizzy and nauseated. How ridiculous! The rest of my family had climbed on ahead, not realising I was in distress. I was more frustrated with myself than anything. Maybe the regular exercise that I thought was keeping me in great cardiovascular shape was a joke. Maybe I had aged terribly and suddenly: how dreadfully embarrassing! Thankfully another woman, although older, seemed to be struggling with the climb as much as I was. We ended up trading stone resting-stops as we determinedly mounted a few dozen steps at a time. How did Moses do this without stairs? Fortuitously my husband glanced back at just the right moment and bolted down to rescue me. Arm in arm, one foot in front of the other, I eventually made it to the summit. It wasn't until several months later that I discovered I was severely anaemic. No wonder I could barely drag myself to the top.

The view was indeed worth it, but where were the railings? My children were dashing around taking photographs—thankfully now sensible teenagers, but scaring me all the same. I consciously stopped and filled my lungs with a full breath of pure, unpolluted air, a savoured gift, since I had come from Cairo. The fading amber sun was just setting, splashing the rocky ridges with dancing shadows that stretched as far as I could see, and glowing with divine approval. What a rugged land the ancient Israelites had traversed! Their whining complaints were more understandable from this viewpoint. How did they find water? Where was the food? It made sense that some guidelines, or 'commandments', were needed for survival.

Moses, Eagle Scout par excellence, had been prepared to lead this crazy crew, but I'm not sure he ever really believed he was fully up to the task. His stumbling and mumbling mirrored his often-reluctant followers'. I wonder if he ever doubted himself, after making it through the impressive exodus escape. I know he doubted God's good sense in choosing him for the task and begged to die at one point rather than face the burden alone (Numbers 11:15), so God sent reinforcements. If Moses had remained only in the pampering confines of Pharaoh's palace, he never would have made it even as far as the shores of the Red Sea. His years of tending Jethro's sheep in the wilderness had laid a strong foundation (Exodus 3:1), but I'm sure he never dreamed it would lead him to the heights of this endeavour.

What an enormous responsibility it had been to facilitate the freedom of his people: doubts or no doubts, he had been given a purpose beyond himself. It stretched him and led him forward, forced him into wandering mode and made him completely dependent on God's day-to-day guidance. Yes, it would have been comforting to be guided by a pillar of cloud by day and a pillar of fire by night (Exodus 13:21–22). I like that imagery. It's obvious and accessible, even if a bit out of the ordinary. Its purpose was to help them travel by day or by night, to point out the way that they should go and to comfort them with a guiding presence. I need that double coverage myself, day and night. Sometimes I beg for reinforcements. Even when the way has become confusing and I feel as if I'm unable to move at all, let alone forward, I can sit and wonder and rest. The light is still there, whether I perceive it nearby or off in the distance calling to me. Regardless, God still gives us what we need to follow, illuminating the path before us, day and night, now and always.

By day and by night

Pillar of cloud,
Pillar of fire
By day and by night
God's guiding.

When life feels confusing,
Overwhelming
Or empty
Darkness smothers my heart.

Yet a path led by Light
Can loosen fear,
Even fear
Unnamed within.

Sometimes a cloud,
Gentle and soothing.
Sometimes a fire,
Raging.

By day and by night
God's guiding presence
Offers light
To guide my way.

On pilgrimage

This last winter, we hopped over to visit Israel and Palestine, and of course it was amazing to see all the historic spots. But my favourite memories come from the places off our planned paths, the nooks we explored and the arbitrary conversations we savoured. In a shop in Bethlehem we listened to fellow Christian shopkeepers tell of their plight behind the towering sealed-off security wall, built to keep them separated from the rest of the world and vice versa. We hired a Palestinian taxi driver who also has Israeli citizenship, to take us from Jerusalem to Bethlehem, and he waited to drive us back. Elaborate artistic graffiti on the Palestinian side of the wall spoke painful volumes of untold stories.

Ironically we arrived at the place of Christ's birth and were given a tour by a Muslim Palestinian, trained at a Christian Bible college nearby. At one point, a concerned-looking Israeli guard in Bethlehem singled me out and asked me where I was from. He asked me first in Hebrew, which I genuinely didn't understand, and I thought he was flirting with me, so I ignored him and kept walking. His voice immediately boomed louder and switched to Arabic, which I at first feigned not to understand. Then he moved in closer and his final interrogation was delivered in English. I had to stop. I answered him in Arabic that I was from Egypt. That got me nowhere. My use of Arabic seemed to confirm his unstated suspicions, yet I never figured out why he stopped me. I explained in English that I lived in Egypt but was American. He waved me on.

After several days exploring the historic winding alleyways of Jerusalem and its surrounding hills, we drove up to the region of Galilee. What a treat! The contrast of verdant cultivated fields took me by surprise, after the terrain I was used to in Egypt. As we drove along, I pointed out a lone green hill in the distance: it turned out to be Mount Tabor, the mount of transfiguration. Biblical history was coming to life everywhere. A thick evening fog had settled over the Sea of Galilee by the time we reached Tiberias. It was evident that we were along the shores of a body of water but there was no way to guess at its size. We found our guest house in the village of Magda (Magdalene), nestled in a valley running down to the sea. This ancient natural passageway led from Galilee up to Nazareth—yet another pathway that Jesus would have journeyed. As we still couldn't visualise the scope of the Sea of Galilee, we asked our host how long it would take us to drive around it completely the next day. Was it a feasible option? 'Only 45 minutes if you drive without stopping,' she calculated. What? I was guessing more like three hours. My biblical map conceptions were completely out of scale. I secretly thought she was exaggerating; she wasn't.

The next morning we awoke to birdsong, fresh air and pure blue skies. Standing on our balcony, I could see smooth glassy water stretched out before me, emanating the calm nature of a small lake, not the overpowering sea I had imagined, able to generate storms of immense proportion. I guess, if I was floating out on it in a small first-century wooden fishing boat, it wouldn't take monstrous waves to make me feel that my life was in danger, though. Apparently the surrounding hills create a basin effect that can whip up stormy winds through the area without much warning.

That day we decided to follow the usual pilgrimage trail,

and eventually found ourselves at the Mount of Beatitudes just as a larger tour group was departing. While walking toward the church and reflecting on the beautiful words of the Sermon on the Mount, 'Blessed are the peacemakers' (Matthew 5:9), I glanced over to see a not-uncommon sign posted: 'No weapons beyond this point'. Just feet away, obediently refraining from walking closer to the church, a young man in jeans and a T-shirt was brandishing an M16 or Uzi or some sort of scary-looking automatic weapon and chatting nonchalantly with his friends. I do live in a police state in Egypt, so it really shouldn't have taken me by surprise, but in Egypt no one has live ammunition clips slung around their necks, especially off duty. Although we do keep our Egyptian church guards as well cared for as possible, we aren't even sure whether the conscripts around our neighbourhoods have any ammunition. If there's ever a real problem, the higher-ups are called in or the on-hand secret police efficiently sort things out.

As we continued our circular driving route around the Sea of Galilee later that day, we spotted the perfect opportunity for a detour. Two fishermen were sitting on the edge of the Jordan River, right near the point where the river flows into the boundaries of the northern shores of the sea. Although our tour books said that the official designated tourist viewing-point for the river was a mile further on, it would cost money and require an extra walk through yet more ruins in the midst of dark skies threatening a major downpour of rain. We voted for the detour, pulled over to the edge of the river and got out to explore a bit. The two fishermen were just leaving with what looked like finished picnic lunches rather than successful buckets of caught fish. They smiled and waved happily at us, which seemed a local ticket of welcome, so we proceeded on our way. An old wooden footbridge spanned the section of the river before us, looking more like an old crossing for shepherds and their sheep than for pilgrims and their cameras. A plank full of rusty nails immediately popped up when we stepped on it. We stayed on our side of the river. After wandering around for a while and securing scenic photos of the green sloping Jordan River banks, we got back into our car and drove off without incident.

The next site indicated on our map was the Golan Heights. Originally we were hoping to be able to stray off the beaten path and up into the beckoning surrounding hills, but our rental car was not legally allowed to make such a detour. So we stuck to the main road and peered up above us, imagining where the exact spot might have been, 2000 years earlier, where the poor pigs of the region of the Gerasenes plunged over a cliff when Jesus healed the demon-possessed man (Luke 8:26–33). Then it was on to Nazareth. Not one person I'd asked who had visited the region told me it was worth visiting, because, they'd said, it was now just a dirty crowded Arab city with a few tourist traps. Surprisingly, it turned out to be one of my favourite stops. Coming from Cairo, I found it to be a quaint countryside village. Again, here it wasn't the site but the human connections that were important. The highlight of the visit was the sampling of Arab sweets, generously thrust upon us by a random hospitable shopkeeper who turned out to know our friend, Archbishop Abuna Chacour.

The life of Christ

The life of Christ,
His Way
His teachings,
Passion, hunger, thirst

Spirituality,
God's presence among us
Calling us
To journey within.

Prayer writing

Life without time for prayer and reflection can easily spin out of control. The chaos of Cairo often disorients me and robs me of peace, within and without, unless I am intentionally living deeply. In any setting of life these days, overwhelming pressures and demands can push in upon us from all directions until we realise the necessity of stepping back from our circumstances and finding ways to commune with the Divine. Using a diary to pray is not just a resource for writers: in this age of technology, it may be a much-welcomed luxury to engage in writing several longhand pages each day, if you can carve out the time. Whether your words take the form of your own stream of consciousness or a letter to God or to yourself, listen. Pay attention. Be honest. Pray.

Diaries are windows. They allow you to see a glimpse within the deepest part of you, and to let light shine into the darkest corners of your soul. These pages (and God) can handle anything you write in them. Try trauma, drama and self-pity. Then listen to the soothing echo of release. This is prayer. Try tantrums, confusion and anger. Then listen and let go. This is prayer. Try questions, hopes and dreams. Then listen and let your soul rest. This is prayer. Try gratitude, praise and wonder. Then listen and let yourself celebrate. This is prayer.

When you take time for inner reflection and waiting, quietening your heart before God, you will see and hear the things of God. Turning your attention away from outer concerns, you will enter into light and discover God's kingdom within. Once your concerns are committed to the realm of conscious thought, visible in diary form, then light can shine on its pages and offer a respite. All witnesses will be present—your heart, your thoughts, your spirit, your mind, your emotions, and God. The words in these pages prove that you are human, alive, for better or for worse. They create honesty with yourself and intimacy with God.

Prayer is a song of the heart, and inside these words will be woven melodies of thought and explorations of discord, creating harmony and a wholeness of spirit, true freedom. A diary is a meeting place, a tool for prayer, where God can fill your memories with reminders of his faithful presence, enlighten understanding with healing, and centre your heart with a steady peace.

Cobwebs on my soul

Dust the cobwebs off my soul,
A negative tangle is binding.

It's not for want of desire, Lord,
But the need for your guiding grace.

All is well

All is well.
Surrender,
Follow.

Yield to the
Strength that lies
Within.

The tipping zone

This morning was a summer highlight. With just days to go before committing myself to another year of life in the concrete jungle of Cairo, I found myself kayaking down a river near our summer flat in the States. Contrasting images of the historic Nile River and this little tributary jumped around in my head as we paddled along. The river being swollen with water from drenching rains last weekend, I had no idea what I was getting myself into. Treston, Britelle, my dad and I had been waiting all month for the local drought to give way so that we would have enough water to shoot the rapids. Well, perhaps the idea of 'rapids' is an enormous exaggeration for this usually tame little tributary. All previous three-mile summer expeditions had consisted of meandering along, occasionally spotting birds, beavers and deer while hoping to catch a bit of current on a narrow bend in the river, to avoid running aground or puncturing our inflatable kayaks. But today, following a torrential downpour, the overflowing banks of the river presented us with the challenge of staying out of the 'tipping zone'.

Treston's paddle had broken in half the previous summer and we had forgotten about it until we were loading up the car to head to the drop-off point. He didn't seem too concerned to have to settle for an old plastic rowboat paddle. Little did he know that by the end of our expedition he would be rowing with only half its length—what looked to me like an oversized cooking spatula. My boat had punctured during that same trip last year in shallow water, but was now repaired with a semi-professional-looking patch. The most common mantra during our floats was always 'Don't puncture anything!' Yet even in the face of my misfortune, I had had just enough air in the remaining chambers to limp along to the journey's end. This year's river height promised us a completely different experience. Water that usually barely reached to our knees was now up to our shoulders. Our main concern was whether the bridges we encountered along the way would be passable or whether water levels would be too high to allow us to row underneath. A final reconnaissance trip that morning to a bridge near the end of our route confirmed that we were good to go.

My first capsize came about as I attempted to rescue Treston, or rather his boat, which had escaped him on a sharp bend in the river. From the vantage point of my boat top, the river's current looked quite manageable. I had spotted my son rammed against an overhanging tree trunk, and the narrowness of the river gave him just one choice: leave the kayak, submerge, go with the river's intent and reemerge on the other side. It worked, but I was still holding his abandoned boat, calling out to make sure he had come through intact, rocking wildly in my own boat as the current pummelled me, trying to keep my emergency mobile phone dry and juggling two paddles. The only reward for my heroic struggle was a very cold plunge, jolting yet refreshing. There I was in midstream, desperately clinging to an insect-infested tree branch, barely able to stand as water swirled around my shoulders. Fighting the current's strength was impossible. The moment I let go of that plan and called for help, my father appeared on the scene, shouting encouragement. No boat punctures so far!

Lessons learned: rivers are designed to flow water in one direction; currents take you wherever they want you to go; fighting against the strength of a river is futile; let go and let the river carry you. Then the fun begins. No need to paddle, just steer. Hopping aboard a moving inflatable kayak midstream is possible—when you are willing to share your ride temporarily with curious local insect residents dragged aboard from their tributary webs, and you stop panicking long enough to concentrate. The journey is more rewarding when shared with a (human) friend, but only offer to hold on to as much extra floating gear as you have hands for.

At one lull in the swollen river, the beauty surrounding us was so pristine, you would have thought we were on a southern Nile River offshoot untouched by civilisation, until the nearby hospital's fleet of ambulances raced by with their high-pitched sirens whining. What a contrast to be floating carefree while, nearby, someone was fighting for their life! It felt eerie. I prayed for whomever it might be, trusting that God would know the details. Then I thought about the river again: the need for help in the midst of our tame little paddle seemed so insignificant in the face of a real-life emergency that the ambulances were racing to meet. The contrast was humbling, yet it magnified the need for help in whatever may come our way in life.

In my own life's journey, I must not forget God's help in the rushing currents, but I still need to expect it, to trust, to be willing to see the hand of God and accept it in a friend's offer for help. So it is with the creative process and the purposeful living of life. It is a process of surrender, not control, of listening and responding, of letting go, yielding and following. Even when the currents of life seem to be taking huge chunks from around its edges and the sirens are blaring, even when rivers and storms seem to be threatening destruction from all sides, it is possible to maintain a quiet calm at the very centre of our beings where we are held securely by God's strength, God's guiding strength.

Simply let go

When the overflowing banks of life
Are threatening your very existence,

It is time to stop,
Step back and reflect
On the purposes guiding your heart.

Has quiet calm been pushed aside
By urgent demands of time?

Today the river can carry you forward
From a place of chaos and rushing

To a moment in time, giving you choices.
Continue fighting or simply let go?

Trust, release—what's holding you back?
The River is flowing with purpose.

Some things in life we cannot control;
Find the centre of your being, your strength.

Let its current carve channels of joy,
As it carries you safely onward.

Join the current of your purpose.
Listen to the voice of your Guide.

The college send-off

Journal entry: Tomorrow I leave home to take my dear daughter Britelle to college. It seems just yesterday that I was cradling her as a baby in the wee hours of the morning, praying that her high fever would break. The forever-clear memory of her gazing with awe into the eyes of her newborn brother, carefully tucking her soft little fingers into his tiny hand, is alive and fresh within me. Other memories—well, the traumas fade, thankfully, as the years go forward. We shared the difficult times of embracing life in Cairo and the ups and downs of teenage years, both struggling through moments of deep depression. Yet the moments of darkness and the hours of despair become lighter in the morning sun. I must remember to pack my Cairo sunglasses to hide my swollen tear-filled eyes from strangers. How can I explain that my tears are as full of joy as sorrow? It is a huge transition, a loss of her constant presence, so close to my heart that she carries a part of me with her, now and always. But it is also a moment of celebration, a dream, an indescribable gift.

I met with a close friend this week who had survived her child's send-off just days earlier. It sounded as horrible as I imagined it would be, but then another friend wrote telling me of her college goodbye under the shade of a strong oak tree. She and her daughter each collected an acorn to remember the moment. At this milestone of life in the sweltering heat of a humid summer send-off, she told me that God had provided just what she needed—a memory tree.

Then I had lunch with another dear friend who had to say her college goodbye in the midst of sending her husband off to Afghanistan for a year. We talked for hours, not of anything particularly profound, just sharing life-stuff. She too needs trees and wild flowers to 'breathe'. When I left her, I felt as if I had just rested by a quiet stream, a place of refreshment. What a gift!

But I can hardly hold the thought of the mother here who lost her beloved son this summer—one of our daughter's best friends. Bless her, Lord, with your life-sustaining presence. What she would give to be able to say only a college goodbye! These thoughts are whirling around in my mind and heart as I try to make sense of it all. Sometimes I have more questions than answers. When I sit with questions until they reshape themselves into glimpses beyond the veil of my material world, then I can let them go for a while. I may never have the answers to some of the questions I ask. Maybe that's not their purpose. 'If only...' is a statement that shuts me down; 'What if...' is a statement that lets me dream.

I can imagine Britelle's college send-off like a dream in advance. Right now it feels more like a looming nightmare. Over two months ago, her college sent us a very warm but informative letter to let us know that there would be a 'Leave-taking' ceremony on the day I settle her into her residence hall. It was excruciatingly clear that, at the end of the ceremony, the students would head off for an orientation activity and the parents would head off for the rest of their lives, alone. But the college administrators kindly tiptoed around our reality. Of course they are there for our children, not for us. I wonder if they'll have parental trauma counsellors on hand, but I doubt if that's part of our tuition package. Maybe I should have attended the generously offered 'Letting go' seminars at school last spring, but I just wasn't quite ready to face it then.

If I am going to follow my usual overly organised plan-ahead mode of operation, I really need to get a plan in place for what I am going to do the minute I drive out of that college car park. 'Cry and then hover somewhere between denial and acceptance' might work. Someone suggested getting lost in a book, ordering junk food or shopping therapy. I don't know yet. Paul-Gordon won't be reachable by telephone because he'll be sound asleep, seven hours ahead of me in Cairo. Of course I could wake him if I reach emergency status, but I'm not sure if needing to weep together counts as an emergency. It might.

Journal entry: It did. What a nightmare and trauma the sending-off-to-college thing has been. Don't let anyone fool you into thinking it is only a win–win situation. It is a 'lost' before it's a 'win'. It has been one of the worst weeks of my life, and I feel as if I have been through a major trauma, completely drained and exhausted. How could something so positive— launching your child into adulthood through a wonderful college experience—feel so completely miserable? The details are still too painful to record, although I doubt they will fade with time. I don't think I will be able to let my son leave home —not for college, not for life. Well, maybe when he turns 65. It turned out that the 'Leave-taking' ceremony was actually called a 'Welcome' ceremony; of course it was all about the students, as it should be. After seeing Britelle head off to her first orientation activity, I started to cry my eyes out, even before I could reach the car. Mums and dads all around me were securing their sunglasses into place; I'd misplaced mine somewhere between Egypt and Minnesota. It didn't seem to matter. I spotted the two college chaplains lingering on the fringes as I reached the car park. Thank goodness they didn't ask me how I was doing. I drove back to my motel and put through an emergency call to Cairo, cried some more, called my parents, cried some more, called my in-laws, cried some more, called my sisters-in-law. And then I saw a telephone call coming through to me from my dear long-lost daughter.

'Mum, I forgot to give you your present,' she said quietly over the phone. Perhaps a police state had already been formed on campus to keep helicopter parents away and she had to resort to a whisper.

'I'll be right there,' I said, my voice reflecting the sense of urgency. Could I go through another goodbye session so recently on the heels of the first? I drove back on to campus, as hunched down in my seat as possible, sweeping the land-scape for any sign of monitoring adults. The coast was clear: a completely deserted-looking campus greeted me. What happened to the pavements teeming with students? I quickly called Britelle and told her to meet me outside her residence hall as soon as possible. She appeared with a beautifully wrapped gift, a mother–daughter necklace inscribed with the words 'mother–daughter/friends forever', along with a moving card expressing her love. I somehow managed to hold back my tears temporarily, hugged her again, reminded her of my letter (the college send-off one) and drove away slowly as she walked back into her new home. She never looked back. I hate this day. Even though I know it is the very best place and thing for her, it was still so awful to say goodbye.

But even now I can project my mind forward in time and see her thriving and happy, and myself as well. It is so vital to live in the present moment, but also so freeing to dream.

— ❖ —

Journal entry: My one consolation came the next morning: the seven-hour drive 'home' to Chicago before flying back to Egypt the following day. I had wisely allotted myself time for a good night's sleep—not that I could sleep, with all my emotions wreaking chaos. But I got up early the next morning, and my eyes and soul were treated to the sight of endless fields of corn, pastures of grazing cows and wide-open windblown prairies. Glimpses of birds perched on fence posts, flocks of wild turkeys and winding river valleys carried me forward. I gulped in deep breaths of pure country air, savoured the sight of rain-washed apple orchards and pristine blue skies, and emerged from my journey ready to face another year of barren concrete wilderness in Cairo—a place I now call home.

Watching over you

A muffled roar blew through the trees.
It was time to say goodbye.

I had imagined this memory so often in advance,
With dread it paralysed me.

As the years of your life carried you forward
You were bound to my heart forever.

Yet the day would come when you would fly.
It was a dream I'd envisioned many times.

But when the time came and I tried to hold on,
Our Creator met my darkness.

Gazing from the window of your new room
I discovered a maple tree grove,

Watching over you, day and night,
Their strong roots full of purpose.

Surely branches would break in strong winds,
And autumn leaves fall to the ground.

Barren winter branches would shimmer
With crisp white snow;

Buds would emerge from their hidden places
And offer you life anew.

It is a gift, a reminder, to me of Life
Watching over you, now and always.

Comfort people

The sudden loss of our daughter's dear friend Tom, soon after graduation, was devastating. He was one of Britelle's best friends, one of our favourite people. It happened while we were away from Egypt before settling Britelle into university in the US. Tom was a gift; he was like a brother to her. His parents were so very kind to let us spend time with them after we returned from our summer away, leaving our daughter to start college—the same dream they had planned for their son. In the midst of their unspeakable loss they were willing to share their hearts, let us glimpse their journey of suffering, allow us time to sit together as our hearts cried one moment and laughed the next at the immeasurable gift of joy that was their son's life. They told us of a lovely Indian archbishop who had led Tom's funeral back home in India. He had been the presiding priest years earlier, at the time of his parents' formal engagement, and had known Tom since he was a young boy. The archbishop also took time to listen deeply, to meditate in God's presence and to offer them inspired words of true comfort at Tom's funeral service. His parents handed us a copy of the words he had shared, and only God's Spirit could have whispered to him such soothing beauty. No words can comfort what only God can console, yet God uses the presence of comfort people. Tom's parents were 'comfort people' to us, a link to the beyond, in the midst of their own raw vulnerable pain.

I think of other comfort people and places—some from

long ago, some more recent, yet all part of the fabric of my life. That same summer I spent a wonderful evening back in the US with some treasured friends: 'Uncle' Jim, 'Aunt' Nita and dear Cheryl. Cheryl is a gift. They all are gifts. Our families have been intertwined for so many years now, I can hardly remember not knowing them. They are like comfort food for my soul, comfort people in my life. Cheryl is a special girl, the same age as me, with Down's syndrome; and Uncle Jim is a dear soul in the midst of a struggle with Alzheimer's. And then Aunt Nita is the one who holds it all together—a living saint, full of inner strength and resolve, and a gifted nurse, very much needed and cherished by her family and friends.

I also got to visit another comfort person that summer, the friend I've known longer than any other. Cindy tragically lost her husband Barry to a heart attack that year. He was only 43. Her beautiful daughters were aged 8 and 13. As I've said, no words can comfort what only God can console, yet just being together and seeing her faith in God's goodness and mercy and faithfulness gave me strength. It didn't mean that the tough questions weren't there—they have to be—but it was her brave choices that I admired. She could see that the little details of life matter, and she was looking and choosing to see God's generous hand in the midst of all the pain and heartache and grief.

When I think of the gifts of these treasured comfort people, my breathing calms and my heart smiles. I hope my life will add to the healing of our world, our friends, our family. But at times I just get paralysed by circumstances as waves knock me off my feet, robbing me of my centre of balance. Rest and refuge are part of our healing in life as we intentionally seek to move toward the centre of our true selves, where God's image shimmers unhidden and the source of all comfort awaits.

There are so many ways that God can pour comfort into our lives, if we are willing to ask and search and receive.

Christians in Egypt take great pride in the fact that their country sheltered Jesus and his family long ago when they were refugees. In a land where history is so ancient and valued, the connection to Jesus, many centuries back, remains vibrant and alive. I sense a collective consciousness of honour in their role of receiving and sheltering and comforting the holy family during their time of fear and vulnerability. God chose to use people along their journey to protect them. All around Egypt, monasteries were founded as stories spread of their presence and oral traditions were devotedly handed down from generation to generation. I wish we had a glimpse into those years in our scriptures. But we can certainly imagine them as they might have played out, because those same stories continue to happen in quiet hidden ways all over the world, when one heart reaches out to another and values of compassion conquer fear and offer comfort. The gift of sanctuary to others, physically or spiritually, is life-giving. Sometimes it may cost us nothing. Other times it may cost us everything, yet gives back all we truly need.

To know the places of inner comfort, in sacred stillness we must look and live and listen deeply. When we protect such boundaries within, we can share with others in need of shelter from outward oppression or inner turmoil. God guides us in our own souls and teaches us to be rooted so deeply that no storm can move us. From the source of life run new beginnings, pointing us from a place of stillness toward what will emerge from our times of suffering. Yet such depth does not only yield itself from the instruction of hardship. It is possible to see heaven on earth with minds that wonder, eyes that see, and ears that hear. To peer through the openings of what

Celtic Christians so insightfully have called 'thin places' is to glimpse the surging of God's essence, calling us toward new beginnings. From the seen to the unseen, the known to the unknown, runs the deep river of God's compelling love and comfort.

Comfort rests

Comfort rests.
It is still.
It is waiting.
In the sound of silence it calls;
The smell of clover,
The shape of a tree,
Sometimes in the voice of a friend.

Comfort rests.
It is still.
It is waiting.
In the melody of a song it breaks through;
The promise of the sun,
The shade of the moon,
Sometimes in the smile of a stranger.

Comfort rests.
It is still.
It is waiting.
In the colour of a memory it soothes;
A treasured photograph,
A loved one's laughter,
Sometimes in the light of a child.

Comfort rests.
It is still.
It is waiting.
In the splash of a river peace flows;
The taste of calm
At the centre of life,
'If only' gives way to gratitude.

Mighty wings

Surround me with Your
Mighty wings.
My life belongs to
You.

The Green Chariot

At this stage in its life I call it the Green Chariot. Sometimes I've called it a 'Mercedes' in jest, but I think the ancient image of a chariot boosts its dignity more appropriately. Sometimes it has been a downright embarrassment as other cars tower over it on the road, taunting it in traffic but rarely succeeding to intimidate. The Green Chariot takes every bump in the road as a challenge and, with great dramatic flair, tosses its passengers up and down like a thrill-seeking rollercoaster ride. At other times I really do feel as if I drive around in luxury when I see the alternatives of many of my local urban neighbours.

I remember my daughter telling me a story about her Arabic teacher here, whose son was complaining about their own 'inferior' car. One blistering hot day, her teacher was due to drive his son somewhere and pretended their car wouldn't start. He intentionally didn't have enough cash on hand for a taxi ride so they hailed a 'minibus' and crammed in like fish caught in a Red Sea fisherman's net, for an educational tutorial. Never again did he hear a berating of their valuable motor vehicle.

Of course, if I'm going to central Cairo, a car is unnecessary as the Metro is a great option, at least when the weather is cooler. We also have an absolutely wonderful 'on call' Egyptian driver named Musa, who will take us anywhere we ask, for a price, in his much more comfortable car. My husband says that Musa laughs and calls our car a 'girl's car', but I won't get into that. We know what he's trying to communicate and we laugh along with him—except when the Green Chariot fails to start. Then blood pressures rise. My friends here with 'big' cars and drivers are generous enough to pick me up when my car is going through a non-starting phase or my husband is off with it elsewhere. I can actually walk to most of the places I need to go, or even order in things I can't carry. I have nothing to complain about.

When we first moved to Cairo, our priority, after finding housing, was buying a car. With the adjustment to life here in the heat of midsummer, just the thought of a mode of air-conditioned transportation cooled me off. I remember one of my first rides on the steaming hot Metro. The first two train cars were reserved for women and it only took me one ride with my husband in the integrated car to realise that I was made for the women-only section. It actually is a lot of fun whenever I am in adventure mode. My first ride in the women's car found me crammed between teenage schoolgirls wearing their colourful head-covered uniforms, heading home from a day of classes. They were delighted to get to practise their English on me, and I my first phrases of Arabic. We were sardined in so tightly that there was no way I could keep a low profile. With the swaying turns of the lunging train car, we all leaned forward and backward in unison. I didn't have to worry about falling over because other sweaty bodies were holding me in place. That must have been when I learned to breathe through my mouth, but, trust me, it was much more pleasant than what my husband was experiencing, several cars along.

The first question I was asked by a designated young interviewer was, 'Where are you from?' I smiled and answered and then my response was relayed by turning heads and delighted giggles throughout the Metro car like a delayed wave of vocal echoes. The next question: 'Was I married to an Egyptian?'

73

The answer that I lived in Egypt but was married to an American brought many raised eyebrows and squeals of excitement. And on it went as we bonded momentarily in time.

So we went in search of our first car. We had never owned a brand new one before, but, following all the advice given and experiencing the rough and rugged roads for ourselves, we realised that unless we wanted to have our car living at the mechanic's shop, brand new was the way to go. Cost was the next dictator and, with exorbitant duty taxes in the country, that quickly narrowed things down. We had about three options in our $10,000 range and a little sage green Renault Clio won out. We had been to the showroom multiple times and found the car we wanted; we were guaranteed that we could drive it home if we paid cash on the spot. In those days, the only payment option was cash. Paying by cheque meant huge delays and car loans didn't exist. A full staff of professional 'counters' was employed by the car dealer, to sort through the heaps of money bags that entered their doors and to confirm 'paid-in-full' status.

As soon as we agreed to buy the car, we were promised a grace period to come up with the cash and were then told that only the 'half option' car was available for immediate purchase. If we wanted the 'full option' car, we would have to wait for four weeks, *en sha'allah* (God willing). Knowing that the government held international transfers to the church account at that time for two to four weeks (for undisclosed reasons), we had already waited long enough to be able to have sufficient cash on hand. We knew that four weeks could easily stretch into who knew how long. The manager quickly explained that the half option car was just as superior, yet with no automatic locks or windows, no radio, and no headrests in the back seat. That didn't sound great but we were hot and tired of red fuzzy taxi dashboards, no air conditioning, windows that couldn't be rolled down because of broken-off knobs, and car doors that often had to be wedged open from the outside. Sold.

Off we went to convert American dollars to Egyptian pounds. Following instructions of trusted friends, we were naively lured into a 'black market' way of exchanging money—an option wiped out by the government soon afterward. That meant extremely small bank notes, and it took a whole lot of them to reach the 70,000 Egyptian pounds goal. Although it was highly unnecessary for our entire family to appear at the dealership for the actual purchase, no one wanted to miss the event. We lugged along our black garbage bags full of money, like Santa Claus on a sweltering summer vacation, with family bodyguards in tow. We were immediately ushered into a private office and offered cool drinks, and the money counters set to work. Several hours later, they emerged satisfied that everything was accounted for. We tucked ourselves into our brand new set of wheels, cranked the air conditioning and drove off victoriously.

For several years, the Green Chariot performed surprisingly well. The first disappointing thing to break down was the air conditioning system. For an entire four years following its demise, our mechanic kept making minor mechanical adjustments and telling us that our substandard ventilation system was the best this type of car could produce. Treston was the first to catch on to the fact that every time we took our car in for a repair, it would present a new problem within the same week, sometimes even the same day. It was certainly good job security for the mechanic, if nothing else. But by the time we had started debating sabotage conspiracies, my husband had formed a relationship with the mechanic, and these Middle

Eastern bonds cannot and should not be broken easily. The mechanic knew where we lived, asked after our family, and waved cheerfully any time we drove by the vicinity of his busy shop. Still, we had to be reasonable. One spring visit for the Green Chariot's annual check-up, the mechanic decided it was time to change the air conditioning compressor. Several days later, a blast of cold air greeted us, filling us with renewed confidence in our chosen vehicle and mechanic. Driving round Cairo for the first time in years with fully functioning air conditioning seemed almost too good to be true.

Yet our current 'car starting' problem can hardly be swept away under a Bedouin carpet. Just before leaving for an international trip last week, Paul-Gordon took the Green Chariot to be fixed, and an obvious wire was found detached—for once, an easy solution. He paid, drove the car home and soon found hot air, not cold, coming out of the air conditioning vents. Then, the very next morning, the car wouldn't start. Well, it did finally start after we had flooded the engine, waited patiently and tried again. I was promised an all-day trip to the car dealer for a total overhaul upon my husband's return, car maintenance, thankfully, being his willing domain.

The day after he left the country, I was driven downtown in the comfort of one of my friends' cars, and the subject of medical examinations and high blood pressure came up. One horror story was enough to persuade me to rush out and invest in an automatic blood pressure machine for my husband. He had had a major medical overhaul during our summer break and had been told that his blood pressure was too high and that he needed to have it checked regularly. Three unmonitored months had now passed by unnoted. Clearly it was up to me to preserve the family patriarch, and this was the day to take charge and secure a monitoring machine.

According to word of mouth, every pharmacy in Cairo was well stocked with them. Just to avoid disappointment, I drove to the largest pharmacy nearby to purchase it there. 'No, we don't carry them,' I was told. Undeterred, I drove on. Eventually I found a pharmacy with one automatic machine left in stock, received a helpful demonstration on how to use it, and went on my way. Fortunately I had managed to find parking on the hectic street outside the pharmacy, but it was challenging to get my car door open and squeeze in and out without being swiped by passing honking cars. I got back into the driver's seat without incident and started the engine. No turnover, no sputtering, no choking: dead. If this was the first time I had faced this scenario, then I would have been more concerned than frustrated, but it was far from the first time that the starter had stressed me out. It was time to pray, plead and bargain in the hope of a miraculous spark. Nothing.

Soon I was certain that there was nothing left to do but walk home, find the mechanic's telephone number and persuade him to come and rescue me. It was a beautiful autumn day and the smoke from the burning fields of the Nile Delta had subsided. I had less than a mile to walk, so off I set, blood pressure machine in hand, handbag strap secured across my shoulder, in search of a quieter street where I could walk unhindered. Armed guards were posted at most corners as usual, and I walked along, avoiding eye contact and the sometimes unpleasant throaty gurgling sounds indicating 'admiration' that often accompanied my lone strolls. I passed a well-fortified street corner and saw, out of my peripheral vision, a young conscript bowing in my direction, not in prayer mode but in just such a mood of admiration, declaring in a loud voice, '*Allahu Akbar*', with intonations that added a very creative twist to the otherwise reverent words 'God is great'. What sort of a comeback statement is there for that? Usually my brain dings frustration at high decibel levels when confronted with lurking lurid 'admirers', but this guy got points for thinking outside the box. I glanced down at my new blood pressure machine. With just the car incident alone, I was certain that my own blood pressure was now hovering in dangerous zones.

Once safely home, I rehydrated myself and decided to take time to test out my purchase. I wanted to prove to myself that I was not exaggerating events, but had been through an acknowledged ordeal. The machine disagreed. Maybe it's a dud.

I searched for the mechanic's number, recorded it carefully in my mobile phone and began to retrace my steps. Oh no. I needed a different route. No way was I walking by that same guard again. Instead I made for the busy, honking street. From far off I could see the Green Chariot patiently awaiting my return. After sufficient rest and more praying, pleading and bargaining, it miraculously started again. God is great!

I am there

My eye is watching
Over all I have made.
Look for me—
I am there.

Search more deeply
Than you ever have before.
In the presence of all suffering,
I am there.

Shout anger, pain,
Despair, longing.
Look for me—
I am there.

In a cry of distress,
Or the sound of laughter
Look for me—
I am there.

Search more deeply
Than you ever have before.
In the presence of all happiness,
I am there.

Sing thanks, joy,
Praise, admiration.
Look for me—
I am there.

Look into their eyes

This morning, after I had dropped Treston off at school, I decided to stop at my favourite bakery nearby. The creative vision of two Egyptian brothers who grew up in America has given us this shop, which has doubled in size since we arrived. Fresh wholewheat bread, bagels and our favourite cheesecake are all part of the draw. But today I was in search of a short cut for the brunch I was hosting the next morning: spinach quiche.

When I reached the baker's street, the only parking spots I could find were filled with rubbish. In recent years, rubbish has taken over our streets. I blame the banning of slow-moving donkey carts in our area, but who knows where the real source of the problem lies? The latest theory I've heard is that our region of Cairo, as a result of the ever-expanding population, has been designated as part of a government district further south of us, and management resources there can only afford to send rubbish trucks through the area once a day rather than the usual three times. We do have faithful street sweepers who work constantly to keep the edges of our roads clear of litter and sand and fallen leaves, but the piles of rubbish continue to grow.

I managed to park my car along the edge of a rubbish pile with only the empty passenger side glued to the debris. I waited for traffic to clear and then got out to buy my quiche. As I was walking across the road, I was feeling mildly guilty that I would have to pay so much for the luxury of not baking the food from scratch, but I reckoned that my priorities could be justified at least to myself. I winced invisibly at the cost at the checkout, but quickly reminded myself that I needed to save time because I was trying to squeeze in an extra writing day, as the following week was a week-long Muslim holiday. With all the schools in Egypt closed for the great *Eid al-Adha*, a festival in commemoration of Abraham's willingness to sacrifice his son, my home would certainly be too chaotic, with the energetic presence of teenagers coming and going, to fit in a quiet period of writing. Treston had promised me some mother–son time as well, during the days when I would be in 'lock down' mode as the sacrificial slaughter of animals took place. My like-minded vegetarian daughter and I had learned the hard way, during our first year in Egypt, when we'd decided to venture out as a family and see what the holiday was all about. It remains a sombre and thought-provoking event for me each year, best pondered from the refuge of my apartment.

Quiche in hand, I received and gave the blessing of God's peace, *ma'a salaama*, as I left the bakery and made my way back to my car. As I was waiting to cross the street, a small pick-up truck, heaped to the sky with rubbish, rumbled by. I often unconsciously filter out such a scene because the layers of dirt and grime build up quickly in my mind and weigh me down over time like a suffocating sarcophagus. Inwardly I then get into the cycle of begging for nature and fresh air to relieve my heaviness, and on and on I go; it's easier just to filter such things out from the start. But today I chose to look up, and on the summit of the truck's rubbish heap was a boy staring down at me. He was probably my own son's age. While my son was at school learning, here was this young teen working to help sustain his family's livelihood. His eyes locked into mine. They were brown and warm, full of respect and courage.

He didn't smile with his mouth, as it wouldn't have been culturally appropriate in that situation, but he did smile with his eyes. I smiled back just slightly, hoping he could sense my blessing and my respect for him. His life couldn't have been more different from the life of my own son, but they were both worthy of admiration, because manoeuvering the challenges of teenage years is never easy. The lingering moment between the boy and me stretched out so long that I couldn't hold back my tears, as I imagined the hopes and fears of this young life that connected with and blessed me, just for one moment in time.

It caught me off guard. How much am I missing by hiding my eyes and burrowing into my protective shell? By paying attention to what an uneventful day could offer, I'm sure I would link in more closely to the daily workings of my Creator. Bless that dear boy, Lord, I prayed, and all those vulnerable marginalised children you've created, young and old. And mine too. They are not out of your grasp. May they be aware of your presence sustaining them today.

I climbed back into what now felt like a luxury car—our little dented Green Chariot. I thought of the times we have visited Mokkattam, 'Garbage City', here in Cairo to see the clashing of hope and despair in the work of recycling rubbish. I wondered about all the pig farmers in Mokkattam whose livelihoods were wiped out after the government's decision to slaughter livestock to prevent the spread of swine flu. Our church supports amazing grassroots projects there, which help meet the overwhelming needs, from educational opportunities to helping the disabled. I remembered the first time we took our children to see the churches in the heart of the area. In my mind, this was going to be an eye-opening experience for our sheltered Western offspring, convincing them of how fortunate they were and how miserable life could be. I was totally taken back by a comment from Treston: 'The children seem happy, Mum.' What? That backfired. But as I looked around, the children were busy tossing bits of orange peel back and forth, and playing around with their donkey carts when they weren't working. We have so much to learn from children.

After securing a safe place for the quiche in my car, and looking in the rear-view mirror to make sure I had dried all the tears from my face, my mobile phone rang. It was a friend in obvious distress. New to Cairo, she was extremely worried about leaving her dog for the first time at the kennel that most expatriates use. Her family was being treated to a company-funded African safari for a week, and she just didn't feel at peace about going. (I assured her that we had only had great experiences with our dog at that kennel.) On top of that, she had just learned that her daughter had chosen the most expensive 'week without walls' school trip being offered that year, but she wasn't positive that the company would fund it again. Her distress was real, regardless of the circumstances.

My heart started jumping around like a Middle Eastern fly trying to escape destruction on a scorching summer day. Yet I kept returning in my mind to the lasting gift I had been given by that moment with the boy on the rubbish truck. The most enduring and transforming gifts we are given are rarely tangible. They are gifts from above, and they often arrive when we least expect them but, perhaps, most need them. Receiving such gifts may involve no more than looking into the eyes of another and truly seeing. If only I could remember the simple instruction that my mother gave me as a child when meeting someone new: 'Look into their eyes.'

What do you see?

Look into their eyes,
My child.
Tell me,
What do you see?

I see them. I see through.
I see deeply. I see you.
When I look,
That's what I see.

On the wings of the wind

Ride on the wings of the wind,
O Lord.
Go where we cannot
Go.

Encourage the hearts
Of your children,
Lord.

Pour out your Spirit
To make lives
Whole.

Silence is a sound

Silence is a sound. I discovered this one winter during a trip from Cairo to see my brother and his family in Switzerland. The first morning, I woke up in the room of a farmhouse, surprised by the sound of silence. It had a ringing, echoing tone to it; it was full of the harmony of an effortless chant. I looked out of my window and saw silence. A white blanket of snow covered the surrounding expanse of trees and fields. It sticks in my memory as if it were yesterday.

Like the silence before I knew the loud chaos of Cairo, so the concept of simplicity used to be an admirable thought to ponder, a way of life to draw on; now it has become a necessity. I've always been drawn to the idea of simplicity, more because of its voice of creativity and spirituality than its necessity. Planned room for silence and simplicity in all areas of life has proven effective over time against the onset of a sort of spiritual asthma, very similar to what physical pollution does to my breathing and psyche.

Longing for silence; the necessity of simplicity. Because I don't ever experience silence, or even a place with the sounds of nature alone, I have come to treasure it—to long for it to loosen the tightness I sometimes feel inside, a bit as if I am a taut harp string, threatening to break. As an amateur harpist, most of the strings I've known to break have not done so while I've been tightening them in the tuning process. It usually happens in the middle of the night when no one is around, and the extended weight of tension wears them out until they snap. Without enough tension, they don't play the note they're created to play and are flat in sound. But with too much tension, they go sharp and eventually snap if they are not given the correct adjustment. The art of tuning our lives to the inner harmony we have been given is a lifelong process, but worthy of patient pursuit.

The Oasis of Siwa is by far my favourite place in Egypt. The rolling Saharan sand sea just outside Siwa, not far from the Libyan border, is at the top of my personal list of 'wonders of the world'. Even before moving to Egypt, I had always wanted to visit the open desert. I didn't realise that the desert surrounding Cairo was a barren wilderness of rocky gravel, not rolling seas of sand. I was surprised, too, to learn that most of the Sahara Desert is not filled up with sand dunes. Thankfully, though, such a place does exist; being a full ten-hour drive from Cairo and with no airport, it is still protected from being overrun by tourists.

Although part of the territory of Egypt, the Siwans take great pride in their own culture and Berber language, Siwi. Women still wear traditional costumes and life is lived at an unhurried pace, completely foreign to the bustle of Cairo. During our visit one spring, we stayed with my parents, who were visiting from central Africa, in an inexpensive but unique eco-lodge that reminded me of the cartoon *The Flintstones*. Its shower stalls were chiselled from rock, and palm tree beams and palm products filled our room with a rustic ambience. Breakfast was served on a second-floor terrace built into the tops of the dusty but flourishing palm grove surrounding us. We had been warned to allot plenty of time for meals, but I didn't fully understand the reasoning behind this until we sat down for a brief midday lunch before being picked up by a guide and heading out into the desert. We were the only customers present at the restaurant we had chosen, and we politely announced upon arrival that we were on a tight time schedule. In due course we were asked to place an order, and moments later we watched the waiter walk down the dirt path in front of the restaurant and disappear. It took us a while to find another employee but, when we did, the cook explained that the waiter had walked into the village to purchase the fresh produce that our meals required. The promise to our children of imminent sand dune sledding was inevitably delayed.

The Siwa Oasis has history—from a salt/mud brick city that disintegrated during three days of torrential rains in the early 20th century, to the ruins of a temple where Alexander the Great was told by a 'seer' that he was divine. I wonder what her commission was on that revelation! But nothing prepares you for seeing the dunes. It is one of those experiences that leaves you speechless and savouring its images for a lifetime.

To see the rolling sand sea in a photograph, from an aeroplane overhead or as a kind of mirage in the distance is an entirely different reality from being in its presence. Feeling the powdery sand between my toes, whizzing down a dune on a sled and trudging back up to the summit in the knee-deep drifts left me spellbound. We learned that the water filling the oasis lake and surrounding springs had originated in the heavy rainstorms of tropical Africa, where my parents had just come from, soaked into the earth, and submerged beneath the Sahara Desert before resurfacing in Siwa. Our jeep was as old as a vehicle can be. The fuel and brake pedal covers were non-existent, yet our skilful driver was one with his car and the desert. With tough and rugged determination we were driven to the summits of sand peaks and plummeted down into concealed valleys filled with ancient sea shells.

The beauty of the dunes, creatively crafted by the wind, was impossible to drink in all at once. I gazed on it in wonder and attempted to capture it in photos, but it has taken many months and even years to process and appreciate it, to feed off the inspiration and refreshment it provided. This beautiful desert of sand was designed by our Creator for pure pleasure and joy. Scarcely do human eyes gaze upon those exact sand formations with awe and wonder before they are transformed again by the wind.

We too, as God's children, are created for his pleasure. God sees parts of us no one else can see—our inner beauty and thoughts, our joys and sorrows, the longing of our hearts; some longings, of which even we are not aware, he sees. He desires to guide us along paths that will bring the past, present and future moments of our lives into the freedom and security of his presence, the essence of all being. Life in all the fullness of the present moment blows dunes with purpose into our souls, stretching them, etching deep changes within, all at the design of a loving Creator. Maybe only inner eyes will see that beauty. Maybe I will now recognise it more readily in others.

These are concepts I don't often seek to express with words, but instead with music, with images, with the rhythms of life's senses in celebration of God's handprint on creation. The divine spark is in all of us. It is overflowing from its source. Sometimes it is found in silence or simplicity, in a moment of wonder in nature or in the eyes of another—the window to their soul. Each one of us is given abundant gifts for the journey of life, some seen and some not seen, yet all presen and to be embraced.

Silence and simplicity

Silence, the sound of calm within.
Learn from the stillness.
Listen.

Simplicity, the will to listen deeply.
In tune, uncluttered,
At peace.

A gift whose source is overflowing.
Seek
A sacred life.

Live intentionally, shelter the wind.
Direct your heart
With purpose.

All that is past, all that is present,
All that is to
Come,

It stands in silence, awaiting consent.
Choose life,
Embrace it
Now.

God's fingerprints

This morning I called the local grocer to order some food to be delivered to my apartment. I didn't identify myself and they don't have caller ID, but at the end of the conversation the man at the other end asked, 'No Diet Coke today, Madame?' Surprised that he knew my list better than I did, I thanked him for reminding me. When I hung up, I realised how much, after living more years in Cairo than I ever imagined possible, I really do love the people of Egypt whom I find in my path, walking by my side, inquiring about the well-being of my family—in some cases even down to our beloved dog, believe it or not—on a daily basis. I feel as if I have climbed an enormous mountain over the years, and now I am getting to enjoy the spectacular view only visible from the summit.

Yesterday I spent four hours with several 'oil wives' (foreigners here because their husbands are engaged in the lucrative oil business) at a luxury hotel, sampling food for our annual charity auction fundraiser next autumn. The Egyptian/Belgian general manager of the hotel had generously agreed to donate food at cost price for the 400 guests we expect to attend. What began as a small church spaghetti dinner five years ago, bringing in several thousand dollars to fund local charities, has now grown to be a huge event, bringing in tens of thousands of dollars each year and anticipated and supported by people from all walks of life, from Muslims to Christians to people who would never set foot in a mosque or church but have very generous hearts. Tickets for auction tables last year were sold out before they were even printed. Right now, six months ahead, we are getting requests for table reservations for next year's event. Half the committee planning members are from our church and the other half just earnestly want to help the needy here in Egypt. It's a wonderful dynamic.

A young adult from our church is currently visiting the 20 projects around Egypt that we sponsor through the 'Spirit of Giving' catalogue, taking photos and gathering transformational stories. Christians and Muslims alike are recipients of these outreach projects, from donkey care for Egyptian families dependent on them for their livelihood, to special education for marginalised disabled children, to support for Sudanese refugees. With undesignated gifts, we are able to step in during times of crises, such as the recent pig slaughtering here, and provide support to those who literally have no material resources.

The woman I was sitting next to during our gourmet lunch is not a part of our church community but commented out of the blue, 'I love the donkey project. I've supported so many now through the church. My kids are totally into it too. If I couldn't do anything to help here, I would get so depressed.'

Last week I walked into a stationery store and asked a question of the owner, whom I had never personally met before. He immediately asked me how my husband was and how things were going at church. Clearly Paul-Gordon had blazed a trail there. Sometimes it's a bit eerie to think that everyone knows my business, but when I walk into the local café and my usual drink is on the counter practically before I can reach the cash register, and all the smiling staff are sincerely asking after my husband and children, I can't think of any reason not to embrace the whole situation. When I walk into my apartment building, I'm told who is at home and who is away by our ever-watchful building attendants, our favourite restaurant owner wonders when one child is missing for the weekly family dinner out, and taxi drivers hand me unpaid bills to give to my husband. The local electrician saw me 'out of context' in a store recently and came running over to greet me, and the deaf man who regularly helps us park our car on a crowded street was jumping up and down at the sight of us last week because we'd given him a few bags of used shoes and clothing. (We actually think he had made it in big with the women in his large extended family, because he kept making jewellery and long dress signs and giving us a huge smile and a thumbs up!)

I look for God's fingerprints generously displayed over all the coincidences of my life. Each day I wake up and remind myself that years of pollution in my lungs will not destroy me, but being unaware or ungrateful for the abundance of blessings being poured out to me daily just might.

A stream is born

Straight and narrow
A stream is born
In the heights of a mountain ridge.

Slowly it trickles
Towards pastures below
Gaining strength and purpose.

Sometimes unsure where the next turn will lead
It carries along its course.

Gathering momentum its breadth widens,
Then suddenly banks on a rock.

A swirling swell of certainty heightens;
Its search changes direction.

Gradually expanding, it joins a river,
Now, winding and wide.

Flowing freely from its birth in the heights,
On the mountain stream flows.

Watering fields, nourishing trees,
Relieving the
Thirst of creation.

Straight and narrow
A stream is born,
In the heights of a mountain ridge.

Arches across creeds and cultures

Our church recently hosted an East–West art initiative bringing together Eastern and Western artists residing in Egypt, Christians and Muslims alike. *On a Caravan*, as it was called, was more than just an art exhibition. Each artist was commissioned to paint two pieces over a period of several months, one inspired by what we have in common across creeds and cultures, and the other inspired by our actual church building. There are many fascinating people in this world and for some reason I find that they often congregate under the banner of 'artists', whether they speak to minds and souls through visual, musical or literary means.

The intense search for new horizons and ways to communicate was clear the first evening we brought this unique group of artists together, as they introduced themselves one by one via a piece of their own art. The diversity of styles was immediately evident, one using bright cheerful colours, another incorporating the dust of Cairo into his paintings to add texture and a connection with the earth. And then there was Dorian. Dorian paints arches. He is passionate about them. His paintings can't breathe without them. They are symbolic and meditative: inspiring images, calming curves, soothing colours. Having moved to Cairo several years earlier, he was obviously engaged in a spiritual journey. His powerfully painted arches stood in contrast to the stark city chaos surrounding him. Clearly, these quiet gateways, as he often called them, nurtured something in his spirit. I knew he would be pleased with the architect's inclusion of domes and arches in our quaint historic church. He was.

Several weeks later, Dorian invited us to the opening of an exhibition that was to include two of his paintings. I didn't want to miss it. Apparently his artwork had been delivered to the 'cultural palace' in southern Cairo months earlier, with the assurance that the show would open before the end of that month. Eight months of delays followed and Dorian worried that he had seen the last of his paintings. Happily, he was wrong.

Directions to the opening event were extremely elusive so my husband hired a driver to take us, as that seemed to offer our best chance of actually arriving. We drove along the edge of the Nile River, heading south from our home. Eventually turning off the main road, we wound endlessly through unlit neighbourhoods and I began to wonder what sort of palace we would find at the end of our trail. Drying laundry hung conspicuously from balconies. Garbage littered the roadside. Smoke churned out from cement factories, the source of much of the polluted air blown our way on a daily basis. We bumped over an old railroad track, and a lone dishevelled man stood oddly in the middle of the tracks, waving at us. The evening was feeling surreal. I verbalised my growing apprehension that we would surely find the 'cultural palace' to be filthy and crumbling, if we found it at all.

Finally our driver triumphed and the artistic venue came into view. My mouth hung open at the sight of a breathtaking monument of architectural achievement. There to open my car door was Dorian, waiting for us outside while having a smoke. He ushered us into the beautiful oriental-styled edifice. Arches were everywhere. He beamed as I noted row after row of arches careening down hallways. High above us, arches merged dramatically to form domes. Red brick and dark *mashrabeya* (wooden Middle Eastern lattice) beams were creatively incorporated into its structure. 'Isn't it magnificent?' Dorian asked. I wholeheartedly agreed.

Almost a month passed before I saw Dorian again. As our East–West exhibition date drew closer, international media began showing up at planned times of interaction between the artists, who were increasingly drawn together through the dialogue of artistic expression and the bridge of friendship. I happened to be seated next to Dorian at a dinner when an Australian photojournalist appeared on the scene. 'I don't like the questions they ask,' Dorian complained. 'They either have nothing to do with my art, or they are too intrusive.' I saw him shoot a leery glance at the journalist. This burly, jovial reporter from Down Under didn't have a chance at an interview. I mentally edited my own questions and probed further into the significance of Dorian's arch obsession. He explained that arches, or gates, symbolised the place between an outer and an inner space, a doorway leading into a world that can only be experienced through imagination and wonder. 'The quiet realms of colour in my paintings are filled with the sounds of unheard music,' he said. I liked that.

Our conversation turned to a recent solo art exhibition we had visited, honouring one of the most renowned artists in Egypt, also graciously a part of our East–West bridge-building venture. The exhibition's theme had been the *Chaos of Cairo*, alive with crowded images of people, cars, buildings and flashing lights. Vibrant, noisy colours had dynamically energised the artist's canvases. Clearly this did not work for Dorian. He was sticking with arches—outlets for emotion, invitations to a deeper dimension. He told me the humorous story of his apartment building's renovations. Day and night, the pounding and drilling echoed through his Cairo home. Finally, after over a year, the work was finished and Dorian threw a celebration. Within the week, however, he noticed large planks of scaffolding overtaking the building across the street. More painting of arches would be necessary, I guessed. 'Back to painting arches,' he grinned.

Soon afterwards came the public launching of the *On a Caravan* exhibition. Our church building, creatively displaying all the art produced, welcomed hundreds of people to the event. For an entire week a constant stream of people from every walk of life visited the church, commenting on the exceptional expressions of common themes, so imaginatively communicated through the artists' work, and speaking of how moving it was to see them displayed in a church. As the event drew to a close, many artists spoke in appreciation of the positive opportunity to engage together across creeds and cultures. Future ideas were brainstormed, a celebration dinner planned. Then came a quiet reflection from Dorian. The atmosphere of the church had impacted him in a way he had not anticipated. Sustaining hope replaced his usual 'crash' after an exhibition; his spirit had been touched and lifted. After the art was taken down, I reread the inscription on a plaque displayed inside our church, a dedication blessing given by the bishop of Egypt in 1931:

The building of this little Church is the right way to hold on to our Faith. It is a place where God can come and dwell: it is something tremendous, a Powerhouse of spiritual Force; a Refuge. It is my hope that this Church would always be kept open so that people might come in and share their Joys and Sorrows with God.

The thoughts of my heart

May the thoughts of my
Heart be Yours,
O Lord.
Guide my path with
Your Light.

Stress recycling in an ugly flower pot

Hidden inside a cupboard in my flat in Cairo is an old discarded flower pot. It cannot boast that its ancient clay shards were discovered in an Egyptian excavation, not yet at least. It may once have aspired to hold exotic flowers grown nearby in the fields of the Nile Delta, but sadly it was rejected for the role of public display, due to a quality of design that I can only call 'tacky'. Inside this flower pot too ugly to display, I have found a secret hiding place. It is a hiding place so well hidden that it has now been trusted to house my most stressful emotions. Very high up in a concealed corner of a dark crowded cupboard, I have to stand on my tiptoes to reach it. Then I can only manage to slip in one crumpled strip of paper at a time, ensuring that I acknowledge each emotional pressure point being tossed away long enough to look at it, say goodbye and, on a good day, perhaps learn something from it.

Stress recycling: 'using a crumpled piece of paper to get rid of stress—whether in the form of a plea for help or the passing off of emotional information overload'.

I think I was raised with the concept, perhaps from church ethos, that it was bad to feel certain emotions; they needed to be conquered and overcome with power and determination. Yet this left me always falling short, running from myself and out of kilter with God and the world around me. As someone who feels emotions on an intense level, whether high or low, I have found the concept of experiencing emotions just as they are, and moving through them, very freeing.

Recently I came across some helpful advice intended for processing grief: it talked of the need to be gentle with ourselves during seasons of grief in our lives. How true that should be. Be compassionate; lower your expectations and demands on yourself; rest when you need to. It is OK to need rather than only to give. Allow yourself to cocoon during times of transformation. Before long, you will grow wings and fly.

As I thought about the concept, though, I wondered if this licence for gentle self-care needed to be limited only to times of grief. As an over-achiever, I'm a bit shaken up to think about it, although I have journeyed through this process for quite a while already. The balance between pushing and letting go— it's an art, not a science. And only I can really know what I need, which provides me with my own opportunity to set the boundaries I need to truly fly.

Maybe, lessons we learn in the midst of difficulties are to be carried over into all of life as we learn to be who God truly made us to be. The more I explore within, the more I learn of the intimate character of my Creator. It leaves me standing in awe of how perfectly God can meet my needs, even needs I am not consciously aware of.

I started my secret stash of burden dumping or 'stress recycling' one day when I went to make an entry into my 'trash bin files'. The 'trash bin files' is a clandestine notebook that I wrote about in *Embracing a Concrete Desert*. This notebook contains entries of intense venting, sometimes in the form of anger, confusion or self-pity. It is for times when stress needs to unpack itself on paper, which eventually finds its way into the trash bin rather than the bookshelf. However, I've realised that there are times when I don't need to write out endless pages of introspective analysis. I just need a simple, tangible way to discard stress in a hurry—to look at an event or emotion straight on, and then let it go in such a way that my heart and brain agree that it is out of my hands and does not need to be picked up again. This forces my stressful feelings into the conscious realm and then slows them down, like a sports replay moment in slow motion. I can ask myself, what is really happening? Am I seeing things realistically or am I blinded by an initial unhelpful reaction or thought process?

At the time when I pronounced my ugly flower pot a place of refuge for secret burdens, several emotionally heavy things had been shared with me by people who needed to unload stressful situations. I was only the conduit, receiving their distressing stories and holding them gently in my hands, completely unsure of what to do with them. These people, in talking with me, did not intend to drag me down with them, yet I found myself getting stuck all the same, and I could not shake off the images of anguish engulfing me. These tender secrets of their souls hung over me in a vacuum of time, until I realised that when they had spoken them aloud to me, God was listening. Where I was supposed to leave off, I realised that God had taken over. Where I could only offer superficial human comfort and encouragement, God could meet them in the deepest part of themselves.

There are so many different things that have ended up in that hidden flower pot now, often just in the form of a single name—God knows the details. It started out just as a place where I could put other people's burdens, like prayers to lift up to God, entrust and let go. Then, when things hit me unexpectedly that I didn't want to harbour or shelter or allow to grow into enormous proportions, I gave the 'stress recycling' method a try. One day it was just the thought of a loved one that overwhelmed me with a wave of sadness, another day a frustrating incident or a misunderstanding. It's odd how misunderstandings can grow when given just the slightest fanning of encouragement. I got myself into a huge imagined tumultuous mess last week without even uttering a word to anyone. All my reasoning was well justified and mentally and emotionally documented. I just spent way too much time giving it attention, fast-forwarding my brain to wild and preposterous outcomes, with myself as an innocent victim in every scenario. What really needed to happen was assertive redirection from the beginning. Several simple questions could have put to rest unnecessary turmoil. When I loosen my grip, calm follows.

I wonder what I should do with all my crumpled slips of paper once the ugly flower pot is full. I hope it will be a very long time before I need to sort that out. One thing I know, though, is that reopening the crumpled notes would be totally against the rules. Just recently I woke up in the dark hours of the morning, wishing I could drag myself to the secret storage spot and unload what was stealing my rest, but I was way too tired. I imagined my troubling thought floating its way down the hall, around the corner and over my sleeping dog, silently opening the cupboard door and landing safely inside the ugly flower pot. I fell back asleep and by morning I couldn't remember what it was that I had recycled.

One Christmas, a friend gave me a gift certificate for a professional massage with a lovely competent German woman here. My friend had told me how intuitive she was and how she liked to work with pressure points. By pushing on the source of a tense muscle, she could persuade those surrounding muscles to begin to stand down and let go—exactly what I needed. This massage therapist also perceptively discovered the suffering I was experiencing from pollution-induced asthma, just by placing her hands gently on my throat and upper chest. I grew agitated. She didn't push me. She only observed and commented briefly.

These stressful situations I recycle are like pressure points. When I find a root stressor and acknowledge it and choose to recycle it, I am telling the surrounding fallout to stand down, to dissipate. For some reason I feel compelled to use the word 'recycle' rather than 'trash'. Perhaps over time, or at least on a good day, I am learning to befriend and use my more challenging emotions rather than immediately dashing in the opposite direction while they inevitably trail behind me.

This reminds me of a concept I was enlightened about during our child-leaving-for-college transition. Experienced college administrators described the difference between an 'emergency' and a 'situation'. An emergency is life-threatening and requires immediate parental intervention. A situation, as challenging and tempting as it might be to step in and take charge in a rescue attempt, belongs to our young adult and is completely within their realm of capability to solve creatively on their own, in their chosen way and timing. It may be time to start adding 'situations' to my ugly flower pot.

Then there is the concept of prayer. Somehow it must fit into these invisible and visible worlds that we manoeuvre between. Whether it's in the form of conscious written words or an unconscious longing in our hearts, the melodies of prayer are woven in God's presence, where the secrets of our lives linger and are held gently, now and always.

The strings of my soul

To lessen the tension on the
Strings of my soul,
I search for the tuning key.

My heart is a harp of finest design.
It calls to be played by me.

I hate to hear it out of tune,
I cannot find the key.

Love, peaceful abiding, simplicity:
Melodies hidden
Within.

To lessen the tension on the
Strings of my soul,
I search for the tuning key.

On children and detours

Waging an inner battle against children and their detours is a really bad idea. A detour, to them, is a lot more inviting than your sensible seasoned advice, a lot more intriguing, and you won't win. In fact, it's a waste of your time. Not unlike the constant chaos of Cairo traffic, you may find yourself weaving through a maze of speeding cars, going the wrong way on roundabouts or detouring down side streets in search of short cuts.

If you ever find yourself wanting to whisk your child off to safety in the opposite direction of a dreaded detour, I suggest you make friends with the detour instead. Try on your child's shoes for the day, put on her sunglasses and look things over again. Don't expect to win over the detour to your way of thinking. It won't work. If you want advice from the aged seniors in your own life, then ask for help. But if you call your father and ask for wise counsel, he just might say, 'Hey, look who is asking for advice on detours—the child who invented the whole grand idea!'

Then you will have to stop and have a long think. You did take detours. You love detours. In fact, I have to admit that life in Egypt, for me, is just an offshoot of a set of intricately woven detours. Clear your schedule. If you have a wide expanse of nature at your disposal, then go for a walk. If you don't, sit down in your favourite chair, drink a cup of your favourite form of caffeine and think things over, way back from the beginning.

Remember the first moment you held your precious newborn baby so carefully and tenderly in your arms? Seeing that bundle of joy, so fresh from God's presence, feeling as if you were holding together all the dreams you had dreamt and ever would dream? You had arrived, there in the present moment, with a heart thankful and full. If that doesn't help, remember your child's first steps, when you cheered at the zigzagging route of triumph he managed while wobbling happily toward you.

Detours, like children, need to be embraced. Who is to say a straight line is best? So what if every other child you've ever heard of lives in straight lines? Remember the time you wanted to soar free. Who was there cheering you on? Remember, you are not the pilot of your child; at most, you were once the co-pilot. Remember, you are not the baby bird flying from the nest; at most, you are the mother bird.

There is a time to pilot and a time to co-pilot, and there is a time to exit the aircraft completely. Try waving up toward the sky as the plane circles above. You don't know what route it will take, but certainly the pilot will find its way, regardless of what direction you are pointing. And if you ever find yourself wandering in desert terrain, you will know how important it is to trust your guide, one who knows the land well and knows how to let you explore it safely.

There is a time to hold on and a time to let go. When your baby bird jumps out of its nest, she will fly. When your baby duckling jumps into the water, he will swim. You can moan and groan and worry away, or you can stand back and watch and cheer on your brood. Is what you are calling a detour a bad choice for your child or a bad choice for you? What do you really mean by 'bad'? Do you mean it was not your idea or ideal? Did things stray from your Plan A? The last thing your child needs is to be loaded down with more baggage. Let go. Look up. Watch the show. You will see a diving plunge, a gliding turn, soaring in flight—sometimes a move you recognise, sometimes a new pattern completely.

Children, like birds, don't fly in straight lines. No lanes are marked out in the sky. A detour, at first, may look like a fated dead-end. But what if, instead, it turns out to be the blazing of a new trail in uncharted territory, uniquely and completely their own? What views will they see from the summits they climb? Give them the chance to invite you along; you may find that the dreaded detour has made you a friend, and admiring your child's courage in following her dreams may inspire you to enjoy an unnamed detour of your own. There is a time to teach and guide and pour foundations, and a time to watch and learn and cheer loudly.

When a detour calls

When a detour calls, allow it a voice.
Give it your full attention.

An opportunity beckons, calling you forward
toward the life you said was your dream.

Will it dead-end or send you the long way around?
There's only one way to find out.

Call together friends you trust:
Hope, Wisdom, Courage.

When a journey awaits, it's time to follow;
in time, meaning will unfold.

Evacuation

The ink was barely dry from a poem I had just written, 'When a detour calls', when a revolutionary detour suddenly hit our lives. One morning the rumblings of a revolution in Egypt stirred the air and the next morning there was no turning back. One day my life was full of coffee appointments, writing and piano practice and the next day it was full of checkpoints, machine gun fire and tanks roaring by.

Overnight my family and friends rose to the ranks of amateur journalists and spent daylight hours gathering facts for further debriefing at night, from Egyptian friends involved in the peaceful protests at Tahrir Square in central Cairo to embassy personnel with what we hoped was the inside scoop. Mobile telephone text messaging and internet lines were cut early on by Mubarak's regime, but messages continued to be relayed to all levels of society through all means available, from calls going out from mosque minarets to the passing of information between apartment building *boabs* (building attendants).

As fresh grocery produce in our neighbourhood almost immediately doubled in price, we quickly sought to secure foodstuffs, fresh drinking water and store reserves of tap water for potential future shortages. Delivering food to those running low used up much of our energy, as embassy families in our church were mandated to remain inside their homes until they could be evacuated. Meal times were random and spontaneous, as our appetites were limited, and managing phone calls became all-consuming. Some meals would find each of us jumping up from the table at different times to answer our telephones and listen to new stories relayed as the events of the revolution heightened. As curfew hours squeezed us into lockdown earlier and earlier each day, we hungrily monitored our one satellite television channel remaining, thankfully an English international news station.

The day riot police in central Cairo turned against peaceful protesters, chaos broke out and the threat of looters became real. Our Egyptian apartment building neighbours amazingly organised themselves into a self-appointed defence team and prepared to protect their wives, children and us; we had nothing to worry about. An ex-military man stood among them, efficiently executing a materialising plan—carrying one shotgun (eventually another would emerge), two pistols and a rifle— not to mention our building's *boabs* wielding large clubs and enthusiastically accepting our son's baseball bat as a back-up.

Over the next days of the peaceful revolution, we observed a growing list of local makeshift weapons, ranging from large kitchen knives, swords, spears, water pipes (sometimes with the taps still attached), a spear gun (for Red Sea fishing pursuits) and what looked to me like a very large lion trainer's whip. Street blockades were almost as creative, from broken-down street lights, toppled police sentry boxes and fallen tree trunks to our own building's large clay flower pots. Self-imposed checkpoints began almost immediately in an attempt to enforce curfew and keep unknown drivers off our usually busy street. I will never forget the sight of our gentle *boab*, Abdu, waving down a car to stop in front of our building as our shotgun-wielding neighbour pointed his weapon at their front window. Abdu checked their papers, made them get out of the car to open their boot and then signalled the 'all clear' by raising a windscreen wiper upright so that they could safely move through the next road block run by trusted neighbourhood comrades.

Because we were advised not to keep our apartment lights on, we could easily see in the darkness two storeys down to the street and the front entrance of our building, from the vantage point of our low dining-room windows. Occasionally we would slide open our windows a crack to hear better, and regretted it the moment we heard and saw our shotgun neighbour pierce the night air with fire in his first attempt to ward off a mob of looters heading in our direction. The next day, we learned that the Cairo Police Commissioner lived three buildings down from us and a determined mob had swarmed his building, looting as they went, until army troops and tanks secured the scene. Nine times that night, looters made a run toward our building and nine times our building's weapons shot ear-shattering warnings over their heads. I had never heard the noise of an angry mob in person before, but I doubt that it will ever fade from my memory. I can best describe it with sounds I've only imagined hearing before—an amplified swarm of giant killer bees, muffled by the charge of a panicked camel caravan. From our windows we could see looters across the railroad tracks just in front of us, running in and out of buildings, creating chaos. Gangs would sweep through areas with pick-up trucks between their marching formations in an effort to carry off loot more efficiently.

The next day, the driver of one of our neighbours showed us his rubber bullet wound, acquired while trying to breach the police station in our area. They never brought it down, that day or ever. We drove past it the next morning, when an eerie stillness had returned to the streets, and saw numerous tanks and army commandos carrying unsheathed bayonets attached to the ends of their automatic weapons. All thoughts of personal revolt fled instantly.

As many of our friends evacuated the country, it quickly became easier to say who was left in our church congregation than who was gone. The Episcopal Church in the US was urging us to leave, as were concerned family members. My husband assured them that we personally felt safe—not an easy task when gun fire could be heard in the background— but we agreed to leave for a while if things deteriorated further or anti-Western sentiment began.

After several days of desperately trying to secure a place for our twelve-year-old dog Pepsi at the kennel, one finally opened up. Our driver friend Musa agreed to take us out to the countryside dog shelter and, as things seemed quite calm that morning, we decided to drive by Tahrir Square (known in English as Liberation Square) on our way home. As we approached the square, not all the entrances were open but many of the side streets showed the first signs of pro-Mubarak protesters. They looked very intense and Musa made us lock all our doors while voicing his apprehension at driving us to the heart of Tahrir Square. We promised not to stay for long, and it was only 11:30am so we assumed that most protesters were probably still sleeping anyway; he agreed.

As soon as we got to the square, we were surprised by the number of protesters already marching around, holding banners, some eating in designated donation places, others sleeping off to the side on pieces of cardboard or in tents. Soldiers in tanks blocked the entrances and volunteers searched us for weapons, with separate lines for men and women. We discreetly took a few photos of a construction crane picking up a burned-out car, with the Egyptian Museum and the remains of the charred political ruling party's building in the background. Musa looked on in concern from a distance until an older Egyptian gentleman approached us, kindly asking us to leave as he felt that something bad was going to happen. We thanked him for his concern and left. Three hours later, violent clashes broke out in the square. At first we refused to believe the news that horses and camels were being sent into the crowds to wreak havoc. We were told that those images were not being shown on the State-controlled news channels; instead, the State television was brewing up increased trouble for Westerners, implicating them in creating the unrest.

The next day, anti-Western sentiments infiltrated our own neighborhood and forced us to consider seriously our church's desire for evacuation. Plans to meet again at our favourite local restaurant for lunch with other church members were still in place. Several people backed out at the last minute but we decided to go ahead and drive over. Home-made blockades still littered the streets during the day, making it almost impossible to drive on anything but the main roads. As we turned the corner, only a few streets from the restaurant, a gang of young men stepped out in front of our car. With weapons flashing, they demanded we stop for their neighbourhood checkpoint. One young man held a home-made spear with a very long, sharp, steel blade, and another an intimidating machete. My husband rolled down his window and handed out his Egyptian driver's licence. Next they wanted the car papers, and then they asked him to get out of the car and open the boot. Their attitudes were extremely serious and the carefree joking we usually enjoy with Egyptians on the street, even with policemen, had been replaced with distrust.

Eventually we were waved on, thankfully, but my imagination quickly shot into overdrive. Once we arrived at the restaurant, we were told that a rumour was going around the area that two Westerners with weapons were threatening Egyptians. True or not true, people were acting on that rumour. Things were deteriorating quickly. Unless we wanted to hole up in our apartment, it was going to be a very long revolution. Stories quickly circulated of people being stopped at similar checkpoints and then blindfolded, taken elsewhere for questioning and extorted for money—definitely not an event I wanted my 16-year-old son to witness or be a victim of, nor anyone else for that matter.

Curfew hours now made our weekly Thursday evening church service impossible and our Egyptian bishop advised us not to hold our Friday morning service either that week, as the protesters had announced that it would be the 'day of departure'. Army tanks had secured Tahrir Square and it was still unclear whether they would use force to subdue the hundreds of thousands of people gathered there. Still no policemen had returned to guard our church. After we had talked things through with the bishop, he agreed it would be wise if we left the country, and cautioned us to pack as if we would be away for up to a year.

Once the evacuation decision was made, our next concern was the trip to the airport, as we had heard that army tanks and checkpoints now lined the route. A generous friend with connections arranged for a secure driver to pick us up—a Muslim who lived in the Old Christian section of Cairo. Learning that we worked with a church, he proudly told us how he and his neighbours were protecting the Coptic churches there from looters. The trip to the airport was uneventful, although it felt surreal to be weaving our way between tanks. The van in front of us was pulled over by a group of soldiers, but we managed to avoid eye contact and drove on by.

We evacuated on day 11 of Egypt's peaceful revolution, and

by day 18 it was over; the iron grip was released and President Mubarak exited the scene. Although a stable future was still not completely certain, an outer layer of peace returned to the streets almost immediately. My husband flew back to Cairo first, to be certain all was well, and my son and I returned exactly two weeks after leaving, giving me enough time to visit our daughter at university and enjoy some quiet mornings of snowshoeing in the forest preserve behind our flat in the Chicago area.

The waves of change had washed away the sandcastle we had spent so many years building, but we finally understand that things of the spirit never fade. Along the unexpected detour we had travelled, we recognised God's presence among us. We all had losses in the process and we all had gains. Many of our friends have not been able to return to Cairo yet, and some never will. I just heard the clip-clop of a donkey cart passing by my front window, a sound I have not heard in our part of Cairo for many years, since the ousted government had banned the use of donkey carts to pick up rubbish in our neighbourhood. A new moment in time is now upon us. It has been ushered in by the peaceful will of the people of Egypt and God's grace. Inspired by the spirit filling Egypt, full of vision and courage, I find that it is another opportunity to pause and look within, to search for an inner transformation in the face of such hopefulness.

Rumblings of change

Rumblings of change stir within;
A whisper of freedom is calling.

An invitation pulls forward a dream,
Faint echoes of fear cease to threaten.

Patience and waiting belong to the past
as the shattering of barriers beckons.

The journey finds voices in hearts illumined.
Boundaries once present disperse.

Within and without, new rhythms break forth,
beginnings strengthened by hopefulness.

The way forward lies within, without and beyond
Stop, listen, and follow.

Lemons for sale

If an old Middle Eastern woman ever tries to sell you lemons, don't bother negotiating; just buy them on the spot. Today I went shopping at a local supermarket and, as I was walking back out to my car, an old woman approached me, wielding large bags of lemons and a wide toothless grin. Immediately I sensed that something lively and out of the ordinary was in play. First of all, this elderly lady was not the usual poor widow seeking alms from passers-by: she showed no signs of economic need. Secondly, her big bags were brimming with perfectly clean, flawless lemons—clean and flawless being rare local qualities. As beautiful as they were, I definitely had no need for lemons that day—or ever, in such quantities. I waved, smiled and wished God's peace upon her, and she returned the greeting by zooming over to my car door, doing a very impressive bent-over shuffle.

I kindly explained that I didn't need lemons today but maybe tomorrow, '*en sha'allah*' (God willing), a polite response often tacked on to expressions of goodwill. She wasn't buying it. It quickly became evident to me that my potential excuses were riddled with loop-holes. God's will was happening for her in the present moment. She confidently and persistently thrust the gleaming yellow fruit into my hands. I attempted a weak but sincere smile, knowing well that I was up against a pro.

As I tried to assess the situation and sort out my next move, I wondered again at the fact that her appearance didn't show any signs of poverty, although she was dressed in high-quality, well-cared-for traditional black widow's garb. The only conclusion I could reach was that she wasn't looking for sympathy or a handout, but to close a business deal: she was a businesswoman with experience on her side. Although I would have paid generously to capture her brown weather-lined face on camera, I was not coming up with any ideas for how to put all those lemons to use. Lemons were her chosen profession and she was marketing a hard-sell.

Then the dear lady's dark brown eyes locked on to mine and I knew I was a goner. I gave one more feeble attempt at resisting politely, but it was useless; I gave up. Slowly I pulled out my wallet and handed over what I knew would be a more-than-generous payment. Her aged smile widened and she carefully adjusted the black veil around her face. 'Double or nothing,' she retorted. I couldn't believe it. I didn't even want these crazy lemons! How did I manage to get entangled in this whole thing and end up on the losing side? I was already imagining my family enjoying a good laugh around the dinner table at my expense, having been taken for a ride by the lemon lady. It would take ages for us to consume all those lemons and they would be staring back at me for weeks. At least they were clean and flawless. Maybe I could give them to someone as a gift? Try my hand at fresh-squeezed lemonade?

If her resilient, playful spirit hadn't grabbed my own, perhaps I would have attempted negotiation, bartered her down to a reasonable price or just climbed into my car and driven off lemon-less. No such luck. This was her game and she'd obviously carved out a niche market for herself—convincing foreigners that they needed large bags of lemons for quadruple the price that the store two steps away was advertising. Business was booming today. I glanced around to see if she had younger trainees waiting in the wings, watching and learning from the master. No; I was her only student at present. Assertive kindness with a zesty twist: there was something to it. She kept her dignity. I kept mine, sort of. A win–win situation? Maybe from her perspective; but after I'd caved in and found myself holding not one but two large bags of lemons for the price of one in my hands, I smiled at her generosity and we both burst into laughter. She was having fun, living in the moment, and reprioritising my values with a soothing subtlety as she bridged the gap between us. I was at her mercy, clay in her hands. In the end it felt very good.

God's image

At the core of all hearts rests
God's image.
Some may not name it so.
Only God's Spirit can peel through such
Layers.
Christ came to model
The Way.

The Creator of Heaven and Earth,
The Universe and
Beyond.
My finite mind cannot
Comprehend
But in my heart
I know.

Everywhere I look I see glimpses
Of majesty and splendour.
Day by day, layers
Within
Slowly lift, granting
Life and
Freedom.

Istanbul

Listen to the advice of your brother. If he says, 'Do not get a Turkish massage when you visit Istanbul,' then heed his advice. I don't care if he's your younger brother, or if he is a good storyteller. He would not come up with such words of wisdom without a well-grounded reason. Do not waste your time finding out the hard way. Trust me.

OK, I do have to admit that my dear sister-in-law, Rebecca, had a completely opposite experience at exactly the same time and place where I was undergoing torture in the first degree. Perhaps I was just given the Turkish masseur with a vendetta to repay, or it was his last day on the job and he had something to prove. I will never disobey my brother again. Years earlier he had related in brutal detail his experience of a small man in a Turkish bath jumping on his back incessantly and beating him to a pulp. How did that memory stay in the blurry corners of my brain when he reiterated his simple warning just before our trip? Well, it came back with full force and in agonisingly precise detail when I found myself lying, with the cover of a very inadequate white hand towel, on a heated marble slab in an ancient Turkish hammam.

Rebecca had kindly offered to treat me to a massage soon after we landed in Istanbul, after seeing the state I was in— barely recovered from a Christmas Eve fever of 103 degrees. My head had finally stopped spinning and I was no longer shivering after forcing myself to play the music for our two Christmas Eve services at church and flying out four hours later on a cheap red-eye flight from Cairo to Istanbul. Sounds exotic? It was not. This is not how a much-craved holiday should be taken. But someone else had generously provided the trip for our family and we were going to enjoy it. My first premonition of bad things to come hit me as our plane was bouncing down to land through thick dark clouds and my sinuses were screaming sharp, shooting, agonising messages. I thought my head was going to explode. I looked over at my husband across the aisle, in the hope of finding some comfort, and saw him holding his own head in his hands and moaning. Our poor children!

Upon arrival in Turkey, I immediately crashed in our little two-star hotel in the old city and slept for as many hours as my family would tolerate. Eventually I was awakened by excited voices telling me to look outside. My children pulled aside the window curtain and the gift of clay roof-tops covered with a shimmering sprinkling of fine snow lay before us. What a welcome sight! I hadn't seen such a thing in years. We were hardly prepared for the occasion, as, living further south in Egypt, we no longer owned winter coats. But thankfully we had packed warm hats. We bundled up in as many layers of clothing as we could walk in comfortably and I wore a pair of socks on my hands. We were fine.

Fine, until later that day when a bucket of ice-cold water appeared from nowhere and was intentionally dumped on my head. I screamed! My hammam hand towel gave way and I could hear Rebecca giggling uncontrollably from across the room. Although she is as close to me as any blood relation could be, my brother had called it on this one. When my masseur refused to understand the English word 'STOP' and kept telling me in a heavy accent, 'This good. Happy when over,' I immediately flashed back to giving birth to my son in

Tunisia and my futile screaming demands, in at least two different languages, for drugs, while my husband kept gripping my hand tightly and telling me, 'You don't want any.' I sure did! I got none.

My loving sister-in-law soon offered to switch places with me and let me experience the delightful and rejuvenating massage she was receiving, but by that time there was no turning back. I started trying to figure out what I was going to say to my brother when he asked me about my visit to Istanbul.

Thankfully, the rest of the trip stayed plausibly within the boundaries of a well-planned self-guided tour. My only request had been to get out of the city setting, so we sailed up the Bosporus on a commuter ferry one morning, planning to hike up to the ruins of a castle overlooking the Black Sea. There would be just enough time for lunch in the fishing village below before returning to Istanbul while it was still light. But we were so frozen after our unheated winter boat ride that we opted for warm soup upon arrival, as did everyone else on board. No restaurant recommendations were made, but only one was not full to the brim by the time we'd stretched our legs on solid ground. We quickly found out why it was not popular—no heat—but the owner was extremely gracious and apologised profusely. He hurriedly dragged huge space heaters as close to our tables as possible and then brought us warm bread and delicious lentil soup.

Shortly afterwards, we started our hike up a steep hill to the castle ruins and had the bad luck of attracting a pack of stray dogs. I was certain they were related to our marauding canine Cairo neighbours, and that someone had called ahead to alert them. They ignored all the other hikers but stuck to us like sentries. Seemingly harmless enough, they followed us to the summit and waited patiently to escort our descent, but upon our return a territorial fight broke out. As we passed the home of another dog, several in the pack attacked her. They pinned her down and she started to cry and squeal helplessly. I began to panic. Our children were upset and my husband took charge. He went straight up to the alpha of the pack and called him off. To our shock, he obeyed. Then the alpha dog called the others off and the injured one slunk back to her home. We were all so grateful she was able to walk, and that she belonged to someone. The rest of the march down the mountain found us staring over our shoulders, watching the reprimanded dog and his followers stick closely to our heels. It was unnerving; so much for a relaxing day in the Turkish countryside. I kept waiting for Mr Alpha to reassert his authority, take charge of his gang and launch an attack on its new human leader, but only docile behaviour and wagging tails trailed along behind us.

Tired, but ready for the pinnacle dining experience of our family holiday, our last evening in Istanbul found us wandering again past the spectacular Hagia Sophia and the Blue Mosque in search of an underground restaurant we'd been told to visit. It was located in an old Roman cistern and had most recently been a car mechanic's shop. I was sceptical but my opinion was ignored. Snow was beginning to fall on the street by the time we found the place. It took a moment for my eyes to adjust to the flickering light of the subterranean eating chamber, lit only by massive wrought-iron candlesticks and a fireplace. Huge ancient marble columns stretched from floor to ceiling, and the surprising sight of a live concert harpist next to the fireplace seemed almost surreal. I looked at my husband to see if I was dreaming. He just smiled.

Christmas always makes me homesick for my harp back in Chicago. We moved to Cairo with only our suitcases, so my harp had to be left behind, but I do get to play it each summer. The young Turkish woman playing the harp that evening was using a Christmas book that I had often played from. I felt a sense of wonder, as if I'd stepped into the pages of a magical world. After eating our fill of fresh Turkish Delight earlier that day, and talking of Edmund and the mysterious world of Narnia, it now all seemed possible. How could a place so beautiful be created out of something as unattractive and mundane as a water storage reservoir? Yet it had. I sat back and thoroughly enjoyed the evening, reflecting on the days we had shared together as a family and storing up treasures in my heart and mind. Some would be thought on and savoured later and some were simply gifts to be celebrated, there and then, by a thankful heart.

Family moments

Moments shared
In the life of a family,
Memories shared for a lifetime.

Some so mundane
They are gone forever,
Some so treasured they linger.

Though time passes on,
What we've shared remains.
All written in the melodies of our hearts.

In them we find strength,
We remember courage.
Acceptance, forgiveness, love.

We learn what hurts,
We learn what heals,
We learn how to love another.

All have shared tears,
All have shared laughter,
All have given of themselves.

To see the worst,
To see the best,
To aspire to love regardless.

A bond of mystery holds our moments.
Share them, create them,
Live deeply.

Water jugs

One evening, in the midst of a lively opening night at an art exhibition in central Cairo, I slowly squeezed my way through the throngs of an energetic crowd watching traditionally clad Nubian dancers and slipped into the calm of the final exhibition room. The volume levels outside had reached such a high pitch of celebration that I could picture my old dog, Pepsi, ten miles away standing at alert, ears twitching. I had lost my extravert husband somewhere along the way, but was happy to have a moment of respite. And then I saw it.

Across the room, a painting caught my eye and drew me in, like the rare meeting with a stranger whom you feel you have known for ever. Unlike its more vibrant neighbours, its colours were subtle and soothing—an invitation to reflection, something to ponder that was full of the earth and humanity and life. An ageless woman stood pouring fresh water into earthen jugs; her feet were bare and her arms were strong. The mud walls and floors of her home were spotless; a makeshift palm wood table held her three water jugs.

I was surprised to see that the picture had not been sold already. The price was very reasonable, but certainly beyond what we could justify at our time of life, with a child in university and another one drawing near to that age. Perhaps it was best. Besides, our walls were already full of meaningful art. It's one of three vices I share with my husband: art, books and caffeine. I wandered away, I wandered back, I became protective, I let go.

Eventually I found my husband. He hadn't seen the final room yet, so I told him my favourite painting awaited him, and then I made myself scarce so that my eyes wouldn't give him any clues. He guessed it anyway. We both agreed there was no need for more art in our home, yet always more need to feed our souls. We planned to wait, to think rationally, to hope someone else would buy 'our' painting so that the decision would be made for us. The next morning I woke up with *Water jugs* on my mind, in desperate need to know if it had survived Opening Night. Christmas was around the corner and neither of us had anything on our lists yet. Then would come my birthday on the twelfth day of Christmas, then our anniversary at the end of that month… Stop. I let it go again.

The Egyptian artist was actually a friend of ours from church and had produced an incredible body of work for this exhibition, bringing to life a people group in Egypt rarely honoured, the Nubians. When the High Dam was built on the Nile River in Aswan in the 1970s, it displaced 60,000 people in Lower Nubia, and they continue to struggle to preserve their unique cultural identity. We now find many living around us in Cairo, identifiable by their darker skin and often jovial personalities. When we first moved to Egypt, it took me a while to realise that 'lighter' skin was preferable in Cairo. One year, our daughter's school photo was lightened to such a ghostly hue that I had to meet with the photographer and have it re-done, gently requesting no touch-ups, which surprised him.

Water in the desert country of Egypt is of vital importance, a treasured commodity. As the Nile River is the longest river in the world and flows some 4000 miles north, the question of who controls its water supply is often hotly disputed. Once, on an extended visit to central Africa, I remember walking almost a mile to a stream with some village women and children to help collect water, as the jungle home where I was staying had none. I slowed down traffic on the well-worn path up from the river more than once, as I was struggling to carry my heavy bucket without splashing out any of its precious contents. Several times, very young children politely slipped past me with jugs on their heads and big smiles on their faces, probably well amused by this crazy lady who didn't even know how to carry water. I became an expert at water conservation that summer, a skill that definitely comes in handy in Cairo when the taps run dry from burst water pipes in the ever-expanding, overloaded urban infrastructure.

I love the story of Jesus and his words to the woman at the well who asked him for a drink of water (John 4). When Jesus spoke of being the source of living water, he was saying it in a time and land where fresh water was scarce. Although the Nile is the main source of water for Egypt, fresh springs continue to sustain nomadic Bedouin, oasis communities and monastic life. My favourite monastery here in Egypt is St Anthony's, one of the oldest in the world. It is located several hours from Cairo, on a vast wilderness plain near the Red Sea, wedged against dusty barren mountain ridges. It is surrounded by a tenth-century fortification wall, six feet thick and up to 40 feet high, and houses an active community of highly educated monks. Founded in the fourth century by the followers of the ascetic desert monk St Anthony (considered by many as the 'father of monasticism'), it is now a dynamic community, focused outward on its numerous pilgrims and on the life of the Coptic Orthodox Church here in Egypt.

All my preconceptions about monastic life were thrown to the wind on our first visit, when our guide, an Egyptian monk from California, received a mobile phone call. I didn't even know there was coverage way out there in the middle of nowhere. He promptly pulled a slim mobile from a concealed pocket in his long, traditional, black monastic robe. Before his conversation had finished, another phone rang, and he pulled out a mobile from his other pocket, smiling sheepishly at our waiting group. Although there is an area preserved for withdrawal into quiet weeks of prayer and meditation, the monks we met were hard at work coordinating retreats, leading tours and letting our children try out what they claim is 'the oldest elevator in the world' (with a pulley system still in place), which, for safety reasons, was once the only means of access into the monastery. An ancient mill, hand-tilled sustaining gardens and a restored chapel containing Crusader graffiti call you into another era. We bought honey made by their bees and drank from the Spring of St Anthony, a natural source of mountain water, flowing freely and linking us back in time.

As we left the monastery and drove back along the Red Sea toward home, I thought about the barren Sinai desert, just across the way, where God even provided water from a rock to sustain Moses and his quarrelling, thirsty followers (Exodus 17). Water is such an essential of life, yet I hardly give it a thought. I am usually consciously thankful for food when I eat, but rarely do I think to be thankful for water.

Fortunately, Paul-Gordon never gave up on the *Water jugs* painting. Because its cost was a stretch for us financially, we decided it would take the place of Christmas, birthday and anniversary gifts to each other that year. It would wear a rotating ribbon to commemorate each celebration that had funded its welcome. Paul-Gordon was out of town when the artist delivered the painting and spoke thoughtfully of what he had poured into it. I spoke of what it had said to me already. 'Timeless life-giving water' was the way he described it.

I couldn't possibly wait until Christmas to hang it up, and

I found it the perfect location. A recently painted chocolate-brown wall set off its frame and blended it into its setting—our dining room. Yet I could see it perfectly from my favourite chair in the living room, like a window to look through, to ponder and wonder and feed from its message. The source of life-giving water poured forth when the foundations of the earth were laid. There is a spring that never will run dry—life, breath, the one who sustains, across the boundless stretches of time. The years are timeless, the supply eternal. May we drink fully from the water of life.

Life-giving water

A river of endless supply breaks forth,
From the timeless gift of creation.

With cleansing rain you wash the earth,
Eternal mystery of life.

Out of your heart flows living water,
Quenching thirst in a desert land.

From the fountain of life springs healing and
    strength,
Unsettled waters are calmed.

Enfold, restore, guide, renew,
Illumine the source of such mystery.

Care poured generously on the garden of life,
Unrestrained life-giving water.

Our days are full of your goodness, Lord:
Boundless, sustaining, eternal.

The weaver of Damascus

My parents were visiting for Christmas one year and were eager to do a bit of exploring in the region. As my father is a church historian, it made sense to find something ancient and with a biblical link. We were also looking for a low-budget option and Syria seemed just the right idea, as prices had fallen because of international travel warnings. Like visiting Russia in the early 1990s, there was no such thing as just showing up at the airport as a tourist and wandering around the country alone. We were not allowed to buy visas upon landing, as we can in Egypt, but all our documents were carefully prepared ahead. It was arranged that a Syrian tour guide would meet us at the airport with our prearranged entry visas in hand and then transfer us to our hotel in central Damascus, near the Old City.

For some reason, most flights out of Egypt seem to leave in the wee hours of the morning, so we arrived at Cairo airport at a ridiculously dark hour and proceeded to check in. 'No visa, no travel,' came the definitive word from behind the Egypt Air check-in counter. My persuasive husband stood a little taller, inched a little closer and explained in a calm, authoritative voice what arrangements the travel agent had made, again showing the letter explaining the approved details. 'No visa, no travel,' came the reply. The next tier of airline higher-ups were called in, the travel agent was dragged from her bed by a relentlessly ringing mobile phone, and loud Arabic rang out in a volley of debate as to who would have the final say. After what seemed like hours of tensely resting our tired bodies against our luggage, weak attempts at humour, and making back-up arrangements, we were ushered through Customs with stern warnings never to make such plans again.

Although we were a bit surprised to find that our Damascus hotel overlooked an empty site full of rubble and stray rubbish, the ancient walls of Old Damascus awaited us, within walking distance. Paul-Gordon had already told me that Syria had more police than I could ever imagine—a network of secret police that would boggle my mind. I never saw one. I kept asking where they were, as in Cairo we were used to tourist police everywhere. He would just smile and say that they were watching me, 'so don't wander off'. We proceeded to wind our way through alleyways, sure we were spotting shadows that would disappear as soon as we turned our heads. Eventually I decided it was more relaxing to be on holiday knowing we were 'safe', without any noticeable guns being inadvertently pointed in my direction as I strolled by. However, our visit was full of friendly people and warm encounters, every step of the way.

The old souk marketplace was amazing—full of colour and the smell of Middle Eastern spices, with nothing like the usual high-pressured sales bargaining that we were used to. We all got hooked on an irresistible local black liquorice that was piled high in bins, fresh and soft to chew. Our first objective was to find the 'street called Straight' where the apostle Paul made his way after his dramatic conversion to Christianity on the road to Damascus (Acts 9). The New Testament records that God spoke to the Christian Ananias in a vision and told him to go to the house of Judas in Straight Street, to lay hands on and restore the eyesight of the legendary Christian persecutor Saul, as he was known at the time. After some minor negotiations with God, Ananias obeyed and all turned out well in the end.

Straight Street, not surprisingly, is straight. In contrast to the weaving web of the old city, this ancient Roman road crosses straight through the souk labyrinth—long and fascinating to follow. We walked past a slanting second-storey dwelling, leaning precariously over an alleyway at an angle of at least 20 degrees. How anyone could live there, I couldn't imagine, but our guide immediately became animated and said that he had shared tea there once with the family and had had to work hard to keep his tea from spilling. A crooked house on Straight Street! Eventually we made our way to the house of Ananias, where it is believed that he baptised Saul/Paul after restoring his sight. The garden held a beautiful sculpture commemorating the moment of healing. Five metres below ground level is a little chapel in what is now the cellar of the house: we were told that it was probably built at the level of the original Roman street. The church still holds services and is the only surviving Christian place of worship in Damascus that dates back to the first century. It contains two small rooms with walls of bare stone, an altar, a few pews and icons telling the story of Paul's conversion.

From there we set out in search of the head of John the Baptist, housed in the famous Umayyad Mosque. It is among the largest and oldest mosques ever built, and one of only a few with three minarets, one of which is called the 'Jesus minaret'. Before the time of the Crusades it was not uncommon to even find 'Isa' mosques named after Jesus. According to protocol when entering a mosque, shoes need to be removed and women need to be adequately covered. None of us had thought to bring headscarves so we had to succumb to a family photo opportunity, wearing huge grey-hooded outfits that we collected from an entry room labelled in English 'putting on special clothes room'. The mosque was originally built on a

Christian basilica dedicated to John the Baptist, dating back to the time of the Roman emperor Constantine I, who legalised Christianity in the region. Before that, the site held a temple of Jupiter. We saw the shrine that is said to contain the head of John the Baptist, honoured by Christians and Muslims alike. It is always thought-provoking, and in this case sobering, to imagine a well-known biblical story in its present-day context. The tomb of Saladin, a key player during the time of the Crusades, was housed in a small garden adjoining the mosque. This would not be the last we heard of the Crusades.

The next day found us travelling several hours to Le Krak des Chevaliers, an eleventh-century Crusader castle, well preserved on a hill-top, its surrounding moat still visible. I had always imagined the years of crusading to be a time when armies marched through areas to take or retake their intended goals, devastating people and lands and never turning back. Obviously that did happen, as we continue to be reminded these days, but there is no way this fortified castle was built to be a transitory camping ground; it was built to settle and defend. We wandered through Gothic cloisters and saw Crusader art frescoes, look-out towers and a massive medieval kitchen. Although it was freezing cold during our December visit, after walking through the fortress until our toes were pleading for mercy we were treated to an enormous feast of home-made soup, hummus, fresh dates and all the delicacies of the region within the towering castle walls, while hot tea and portable room heaters did their best to thaw us out. If I had ever imagined Camelot's Knights of the Round Table with a romantic view, I was no longer doing so. 'Harsh' is the only word that came to mind.

The final stop on our field trip outside Damascus brought us to the villages of Saidnaya and Maaloula, where Christians and Muslims have preserved the ancient language spoken by Christ—Aramaic. We heard the Lord's Prayer recited in Aramaic in one of the churches and then climbed through an aged but active convent wedged into sheer rocky mountain cliffs. An icon of the Virgin Mary, purportedly painted by Saint Luke, was one of several places of pilgrimage there, sought out by both Christians and Muslims. Monasteries, convents, churches, stone grottos and clay houses overlook olive groves and orchards in the valley below. The whole experience seemed a bit surreal. By late afternoon my brain was exhausted by jumping between cultures and centuries, and pondering how seamlessly Christians and Muslims were working and living together.

Cold fresh air jolted me back to clear thinking when I stepped out of our van and stretched my legs as we arrived back in Damascus just after dark. After explaining to the hotel manager our desire to revisit the souk, we were granted approval for free rein. So, with flashlights blazing and clandestine glances over our shoulders, we wound our way through alleyway twists and turns and short cuts we had learned the previous day, and emerged back into the bustling covered marketplace. After indulging in yet more hummus and fresh dates and all the delicacies of the region, we decided to step into an eclectic antique shop in the heart of the souk, whose windows were crammed full of art and silver and handmade oriental carpets. While I was unsuccessfully negotiating to buy a silver cylinder case that I was told was used to carry secret messages in times past, my children found a rug weaver in action. After daydreams of medieval castles and knights on cold errands, it was hard to let go of my unattainable gadget, but eventually I gave up my bargaining and joined my children.

I was immediately mesmerised by the weaver. He hardly

took note of us and kept steadily at his work. He was not weaving from a visible pattern: perhaps it was laid out ahead in his mind, perhaps not. Dark red wool dominated his artistic landscape of shapes and patterns. Rarely do I look at the knotted side of a carpet, but it was intriguing to see the underside so visibly displayed. As if the knots were deliberately trying to get my attention, I was lulled into the rhythm of his weaving. I felt as if I was watching a musician play from his heart, full of feeling and with a measured cadence. The knots reminded me of notes in a musical score, all holding purpose and a part of the whole. It was obvious how essential they were to binding the entire carpet together. The opposite side looked so much more colourful, smooth and thoughtfully designed, yet the knotted side almost made more sense of the chaos. Each knot was part of a moment in time, securely fastened into place by the experienced hands of the weaver.

Just as life has a master weaver who holds the design, each moment in our lives is a part of the whole. With heart and mind we are woven and created, from one day to the next until the day of completion. The weaver is attentive to each movement of his hands, not interfering when the pulsing tempo has set its pace, yet remaining present all along. Some moments in life may never be understood fully without stepping back to see the whole. We must learn to trust in the whole as we live in the middle; we can be confident that we can entrust the details of our lives into the hands of the Master.

The loom of life

Upon the loom of life is woven
Work of the master weaver.

Ancient stories, modern lives
Connected by the thread of time.

Trusting, hoping, following faithfully
The pulse of life is bound.

Colours, patterns, rhythms, themes,
We look to the hand of our master.

What will emerge in the fullness of time?
A life work that is you.

Celebrating You

Creator God,
You know all my needs.
You see the path I must walk:

Light, salvation, freedom, life,
Guiding grace and love.

The magnet of my heart must follow
When fear sets in:
Trust.

Never have You let me go,
Whether dark or light the path.

Ground of all being:
Faithfulness.
Essence of all life.

Christ within, Christ without,
Christ in You and all.
Holy Spirit, light.

Compassion, love, a glimpse of Heaven
Embracing Your image within.

To journey forward is my calling;
To celebrate
Your image in others.

Thank you for Your guiding wisdom.
You know my heart's desires.

Keep me faithful to why I was created.
Lead me on in
Joy.

God's breath

God's Spirit, God's breath,
Gently stirring
Within.
Will I take notice, turn my head,
Allow God's nudging
To engage my
Heart?

Group discussion questions

1. Were you glad you took the time to read *Embracing Dusty Detours*? If so, why?
2. What do you think the author's motivation was in writing this book?
3. What surprised you about the book?
4. Was there a chapter you especially appreciated or related to more than others?
5. What did you expect to learn from reading the book, and were your expectations met?
6. How did reading *Embracing Dusty Detours* change any of your preconceptions about the Middle East, Islam or Christianity?
7. What role do you think the poems play at the conclusion of each reflection? Did you resonate with one more than others?
8. How can picturing the Bible in its Middle Eastern context bring it to life in our modern-day context?
9. Reflecting on your own life, how has it followed the course you imagined? How have you experienced God's guiding presence along your journey?
10. Are there any 'dusty detours' in your own life that you have embraced or would like to embrace?
11. Were you raised in a different expression of faith from the one you currently follow? If so, what have been the positive aspects of the change?
12. How do you think the fact that the author was raised in another culture contributes to her worldview?
13. In what ways, if any, do you think the book raises controversial issues?
14. What is original about this book? How does it distinguish itself from other books you have read on the subject?
15. If you could add a chapter to the book, what would it be about?
16. Have you read Lynne Chandler's first book, *Embracing a Concrete Desert: A spiritual journey towards wholeness*? If so, in what ways does it differ from *Embracing Dusty Detours*?

Also by Lynne Chandler

Embracing a Concrete Desert

A spiritual journey towards wholeness

I wish I could say that I have arrived and will never have to stare into the darkness again, but I know that isn't so. I do know, though, that I have to embrace the present moment and celebrate life, whatever that may involve today. My Creator is alive within and throughout this amazing world, and has never failed to wrap me in wings of protection and comfort. There are many layers of negativity to be peeled back so that a glimpse of God's image can show through. Just as one layer is lifting, another appears to take its place. That's where grace comes in…

This is the story of an unfinished journey—a journey that finds a path through struggle and difficulty to acceptance and peace of mind. It is the story of one woman choosing to seek serenity in the midst of struggles to adapt to a very different life, and discovering how, in the driest of desert places, God can reveal fresh water springs for the soul. It is a story shared through lyrical journal reflections and poems sparked by the ups and downs of life in a teeming Middle Eastern metropolis.

ISBN 978 1 84101 686 3   £5.99
Available from your local Christian bookshop or direct from BRF: please visit www.brfonline.org.uk.

Enjoyed

this book?

Write a review—we'd love to hear what you think.
Email: reviews@brf.org.uk

Keep up to date—receive details of our new books as they happen.
Sign up for email news and select your interest groups at:
www.brfonline.org.uk/findoutmore/

Follow us on Twitter @brfonline

By post—to receive new title information by post (UK only), complete the form below and post to: BRF Mailing Lists, 15 The Chambers, Vineyard, Abingdon, Oxfordshire, OX14 3FE

Your Details	
Name _____	
Address_____	
_____	
Town/City _____ Post Code _____	
Email_____	

Your Interest Groups (*Please tick as appropriate)	
☐ Advent/Lent	☐ Messy Church
☐ Bible Reading & Study	☐ Pastoral
☐ Children's Books	☐ Prayer & Spirituality
☐ Discipleship	☐ Resources for Children's Church
☐ Leadership	☐ Resources for Schools

Support your local bookshop
Ask about their new title information schemes.